Inglefield
Retirement Solutions

To learn more about how I can
help you plan for a financially
successful retirement...

Contact me at:
chuck@iRetirementSolutions.com

Or visit:
www.iRetirementSolutions.com

11111 Carmel Commons Blvd.
Suite 460
Charlotte, NC 28226
phone 704.900.5779
fax 704.900.7525
toll-free 855.407.3175

Securities & Financial Planning offered
through LPL Financial, a Registered
Investment Advisor, Member FINRA/SIPC

HOLY COW, YOU'RE RETIRING!

Don't Let Your Financial Freedom Turn Into a Financial Free-Fall

I'M RETIRED!

Chuck Inglefield

Printing History
Edition One, March 2011
ISBN: 978-0-6154662-6-2

Holy Cow, You're Retiring!
*Don't Let Your Financial Freedom
Turn Into a Financial Free-Fall*

Disclaimer

This book is intended solely for educational purposes. This book uses examples based upon hypothetical rates of return and in no way intends to imply that these represent real, historic or projected future rates of return that have been available in the past, are available now, or will be available in the future from any particular security or investment product or investment strategy. The examples are presented to emphasize the mathematical concepts behind designing a retirement withdrawal strategy.

The examples provided are purely hypothetical and do not represent any specific investment or security. Further, no specific investment or security is recommended or endorsed by the author. No strategy assures success or protects against loss. Individuals should consult with a Financial Advisor to determine the suitability and appropriateness of any security, investment, or investment strategy. Although all effort has been made for thoroughness, the author does not warrant the completeness or accuracy of the information contained in this book. All information is provided on an "as-is" basis.

Dedicated with love to my wife, Meg, who unfailingly brings out my best; and to my mother and father, who provided me with the opportunity and encouragement to create my own path.

Also to the many friends, who first gave me their trust as clients. Thank you.

Table Of Contents

Why I Wrote This Book

I quit!

The idea for this book rolled around in my head for several years before I made the decision to act on it, but it was born on one particular day. I remember it clearly: That was the day I decided to quit the personal financial planning business.

After 12 years of building a successful financial planning practice, I had had enough. My frustration that day was the direct result of two meetings — one with a client, and one with a potential client. They were both seeking advice about retirement planning. The meetings had ended the same way, with both individuals making decisions, against my advice, that I knew would ultimately create financial hardships for them.

Why was this happening? Couldn't these people see that I was trying to help?

My frustration was initially focused on these two retirees. But it wasn't long before I began to blame myself. Why wasn't I more persuasive? Maybe I needed to take classes or read books to become a better salesperson.

I knew something was seriously wrong here. I wasn't a salesperson, I was a financial consultant — a planner. The idea of "selling" a client on a financial solution that was in his or her best interest was not only foreign to me, it was unsettling. If this was what the financial planning business was about, then I needed to do something different.

I drove home that day, considering what else I might do with the rest of my life.

But then it hit me. These retirees had made the wrong choices because they didn't understand — they couldn't see — the eventual outcome and impact of their decisions. I had produced hundreds of plans and analyses of situations just like theirs, so I knew exactly how things would unfold. My mistake was assuming that they could see the consequences of their actions as clearly as I could.

I didn't need to become a better salesperson at all. I needed to become a better storyteller. If retirees couldn't clearly see their futures, then I needed to create a vivid mental picture to help them understand the impact of their financial decisions. That was it — I needed to write a book.

Faced with the choice of finding a new career or writing this book, I knew it was a no-brainer. You're now holding in your hands the reason that I'm still in the financial planning business.

I couldn't quit.

Because the truth is, I love helping people make smart financial decisions. *Holy Cow, You're Retiring!* is the true story of what it takes to create a financially successful retirement.

Note to Readers

Here's the lowdown on special features you'll find in this book.

About Insights from a Focus Group

Here I was, writing a book about retirement, when I hadn't yet experienced that stage of life myself. This seemed a bit inauthentic to me, so I devised a plan. I called on my retired clients and their friends to help me populate a series of focus groups. My goal was to understand the true story of retirement — not just what I imagined it to be.

As I test-drove some of the concepts from this book, I was interested in learning not only about financial issues, but about lifestyle dynamics too. These retirees gave me valuable insights about how the non-financial-planner brain thinks about the issues of retirement.

Throughout this book, you'll learn what these folks had to say about many of the concepts presented. And you'll be able to compare your reactions with theirs.

ABOUT A CLIENT STORY

One of the best ways to succeed at a new endeavor is to hear how other people have done it. We can learn from their successes, of course, and we can sometimes learn even more from their mistakes. From time to time, I'll share a client story with you so you can do that.

About Cow Chips

I'll be dropping a few choice Cow Chips throughout *Holy Cow, You're Retiring!* Read on if you're wondering, "Why 'cow chips?'" All will become clear in Chapter 1.

What are Cow Chips?

In this case, they're facts that aren't worth one red cent, but are kind of fun to throw around. Speaking of which, did you know that the town of Beaver, Oklahoma is the Cow Chip Throwing Capital of the World? And in case you're wondering, the current distance record is 182 feet, 3 inches.

About Facts, Tables, Graphs, Quotes, etc.

To add to your understanding and enjoyment of this important financial planning information, you'll find a number of pertinent facts, quotes, statistics, and other data in the chapters ahead.

Watch For Falling Cows

Planning for a Financially Successful Retirement

FACT: In August, 2009, in the village of Lauterbrunnen, Switzerland, 28 Swiss cows plunged off a cliff with fatal results.

This puzzling and provocative headline popped up on my computer screen just as I began research for writing this book. What an irresistible distraction. I simply *had* to click the link and check out this story.

> **"** Police **baffled** as dozens of 'suicidal' **cows** throw themselves off **cliff** in the Alps. **"**
>
> UK DAILY MAIL[1]

I read further. Were these Swiss kamikaze cows? The scientists interviewed in the article claimed that animals are incapable of committing suicide. Naturally, that begged the question: *Why* did the cows go off the mountain cliff?

Answering this would require further investigation. Like any good financial planner-turned-writer, I wasn't about to miss an opportunity to turn curiosity into a full-fledged morning of procrastination. And my research uncovered an interesting fact: The incident in Switzerland was *not* unique.

> **FACT:** In the exact same month, in the exact same year more than 30 Californian cows went over a cliff and met their demise on the rocky Fresno Riverbed.[2]

> **FACT:** Not quite two years earlier, a cow used the minivan of Charles and Linda Everson to break a 200-foot fall off a cliff in the state of Washington. The Everson's survived, the cow and their minivan did not.[3]

But none of these stories mentioned *why* the cows dived off the mountain cliffs.

What we had here, my friends, was a procrastinator's dream! I mean, who could write at a time like this? Who could let this mystery go unsolved? Maybe I could learn something that would prevent future cliff-diving incidents and ultimately save hundreds or thousands of cows.

Okay…maybe that was going too far, but at least I could satisfy my curiosity — and in the process, avoid the fact that I had no idea how to begin writing my book about living a financially successful retirement.

Two hours into my online search, I hit pay dirt. A three-page document titled "Cattle Handling Pointers" held the answer. This guide for the newbie cattle handler stated: "Cattle can see everywhere but directly behind them or a small blind spot in front of them."[4]

Aha! A blind spot in front of them...of course! It made perfect sense. Cows' eyes are set so far to the sides that they can't see directly ahead. Up there on the mountain, they had no idea they were about to walk off the edge of the cliff. And, it was safe to assume that if other cows were following behind (as cows tend to do), then the whole herd made the same mistake and hurtled down to its death.

Mystery solved...a morning well spent. Time for lunch.

Is There a Lesson Here?

As I munched on my cheeseburger, I couldn't get those poor cliff-diving cows off my mind. What a terrible way to go. But then, they probably didn't know what was happening to them on the way down. I comforted myself with the idea that they were as clueless as Wile E. Coyote (of Road Runner cartoon fame) when it came to understanding gravity. Those cows simply had no idea that they'd be hitting the ravine in a big bovine cloud of dust.

And then it came to me.

As I mentioned in "Why I Wrote This Book," I was frustrated with two clients who refused to accept my advice about the best plan for financing their retirements. I began to detect some strange similarities between those two individuals and those ill-fated cows. Yes. I was definitely onto something here.

Like the cows, these retirees had made poor decisions and chosen dangerous paths because they had *blind spots* — they couldn't see where their actions were leading them.

Aha! The morning spent researching the mystery of the falling cows seemed to have been instructive after all.

Beware: Retiree Blind Spots

Many of today's retirees have blind spots when it comes to seeing the future outcome of their actions. As a result, they're making planning decisions about their retirements that will lead to financial hardship; they're ready to walk right off a mountain cliff. And just like the cows, they don't have any idea that disaster awaits them. Usually, by the time retirees realize their mistakes, it's too late to correct them; their lifestyles have already suffered the consequences.

Unfortunately, this is an all too common reality. The fact is, retirees are going off the cliff in record numbers. According to a 2010 study by the Employee Benefit Research Institute, almost half of all baby boomers are expected to run out of money during their retirement years.[5] This represents a mighty big herd of cliff-diving cows.

But you don't have to follow the herd! You can change your fate with some simple planning — planning that adjusts for your blind spots so that you can enjoy a financially successful retirement.

What *is* a financially successful retirement, anyway?

Insights from a Focus Group

I asked a number of retirees in my focus groups this question: "How would you define a financially successful retirement?" Here's what they said:

- "Maintaining my standard of living."
- "Not worrying about money."
- "Having something left to leave my kids."
- "Never running out of money."

The group decided that the last answer summed things up pretty well. "Never running out of money" was really at the core of all the retirees' responses. So let's stick with that definition for now:

Living a financially successful retirement means never running out of money. Does that sound good to you?

> Living a financially successful retirement
> means never **running** out of money.

Actually, this was originally going to be the basic premise of *Holy Cow, You're Retiring!*. But early in the writing process, I realized that "never running out of money" really isn't good enough. A financially successful retirement requires more. Our definition can be made better...much better.

Consider this simple modification:

> Living a financially successful retirement
> means never **beginning** to run out of money.

This may seem like a petty distinction, but it makes all the difference in the world when it comes to developing an effective financial strategy. To understand the critical difference between "never running out of money" and "never *beginning* to run out of money," let's talk about the mountain where all those newsworthy cows took a tumble off the cliff.

The Retirement Mountain

Think for a moment about what a mountain symbolizes...

A solid foundation. Stability. Standing the test of time.

And consider the amazing views. Experiencing life from this higher elevation is inspiring. What an exciting feeling of freedom and independence!

The mountain is actually a great metaphor for what a successful retirement is all about. Knowing you have a solid financial foundation gives you confidence about your retirement. Having a plan that you know will stand the test of time gives you confidence to go out and enjoy the views that retirement offers — spending time with grandchildren, traveling the world, volunteering for a worthwhile cause, or reading as many books as you please.

Opportunity   Freedom
Confidence   Stability
Independence   Happiness

The views are whatever you want them to be.

Your retirement mountain represents financial stability and
the quality of life that brings you happiness. It represents the
freedom and independence to take advantage of new opportunities.
You certainly don't want to lose — or more accurately, *begin* to
lose — any of these.

The secret to a financially successful retirement is never *beginning*
to run out of money…never setting foot (or hoof) off the cliff.
That's because once you *begin* to run out of money, you're like
the cow falling off the mountain. You suddenly lose the financial
stability and quality of life that the mountain offered.

Going off the cliff has irreversible consequences. You are officially
on your way down. Your descent may be fast or slow, but once you
begin to run out of money in retirement, it's inevitable — you *will*
run out of money.

And you've probably already guessed what running out of money
looks like: It's a frightening financial free-fall…and the end is never
pretty. The day you go broke, you hit rock bottom. Ouch.

Smarter than Cows

It's true that cows don't voluntarily walk off mountain cliffs — blind spots are to blame for these mishaps. And it's also true — if you're like the great majority of retirees — that you have blind spots too. When it comes to planning for retirement, most people have two blind spots…and they are major ones. But fortunately, we're all smarter than cows. And once you learn what these blind spots are, you can make the proper adjustments and choose your path — a path that won't send you plummeting off the retirement mountain.

Using clear vision to choose the right path (withdrawal strategy) that keeps you on your mountain

So, how do you choose the right path? Well, that involves looking closely at the three most common paths out there — namely, the **three** common *withdrawal strategies* that are available to retirees. A withdrawal strategy is a specific plan for taking an income from your retirement savings. Once you understand exactly how withdrawal strategies work, you'll see how choosing the wrong one can lead you straight off the retirement mountain cliff.

On the other hand, creating the right withdrawal strategy and managing it properly throughout your retirement will keep you right where you belong — stationed on the mountain, where you never, ever begin running out of money.

Withdrawal (W/D) Strategy

A **withdrawal strategy** *is a plan or method for taking an income from your* **retirement savings.** *The objective of a good withdrawal strategy is to create a predictable and reliable income. There are different philosophies and different ways to compute when and how much money to take out; however, regardless of the strategy chosen, retirees either withdraw:*

1. **a specific dollar amount**
or
2. **a specific percentage**

from their retirement savings.

By the end of this book, you'll have learned everything you need to know to choose and maintain the best withdrawal strategy for you.

Retirement Savings

For the purposes of this book, **retirement savings** *refers to any investments, retirement accounts (IRA's, 401(k)'s, etc.), savings accounts, or brokerage accounts that you intend to use to create an income in retirement. It's your* **nest egg.** *It's the sum of money that will give you a steady paycheck after you retire.*

Not all of your savings are considered **retirement savings.** *For example, you should always have some money set aside in a savings or money market account for unexpected expenses. Because these cash reserves won't be used to create an income, they aren't* **retirement savings.**

The Grass is Always Greener...

Maybe you're asking yourself: "What are cliff-diving cows doing up on mountains in the first place?" Good question.

Cows search for grasses that grow at high elevations because these mountain grasses have more nutrients than any other vegetation. High altitude grazers actually produce the world's healthiest milk, cheese, and beef.

The Right Path: 3 Steps for Never Beginning to Run Out of Money

The formula for never beginning to run out of money in retirement involves three basic steps:
1. Know your blind spots.
2. Choose a withdrawal strategy that adjusts for these blind spots.
3. Manage your withdrawal strategy appropriately.

Holy Cow, You're Retiring! covers each of these steps in detail.

Part 1 of this book reveals the two major blind spots that most retirees don't realize they have. Once you become aware of these blind spots, you'll be able to choose a path that doesn't lead you off the retirement mountain cliff. Understanding your blind spots is critical for choosing the right withdrawal strategy.

Part 2 is a look at the three most common withdrawal strategies — the two that don't work, as well as the one that does. You'll see how the right withdrawal strategy adjusts for your blind spots and keeps you on the mountain.

Part 3 will introduce a powerful tool to help you determine how much you can withdraw from your retirement savings at the beginning of your retirement, as well as each year after that. You'll also learn a simple strategy for managing your withdrawal strategy appropriately throughout changing economic conditions so you can be confident that you'll never begin running out of money.

Along the way, you'll read stories of successful and not-so-successful retirees and find sometimes odd, often fascinating facts and tidbits.

My goal is to help you understand your blind spots and make the proper adjustments in your financial planning before you venture anywhere near the cliff's edge. I may not be able to prevent future cliff-diving incidents for hapless cows, but maybe I *can* help save you from your own disastrous plunge.

So, let's get started.

Know Your Blind Spots

Part 1

Just like cows, many retirees (and retirees-to-be) have blind spots. These blind spots keep you from choosing the best withdrawal strategy for retirement, and even fool you into thinking you've chosen the right withdrawal strategy when, in fact, you're headed straight off the retirement mountain.

We know where a cow's blind spots are — directly in front of and behind it — but do you have them too? And if so, where are yours? To find them, we'll have to do some investigation.

We'll know if you have blind spots by the way that you answer two basic questions. It's no coincidence that these are the same questions that lay the foundation for creating an effective withdrawal strategy for retirement:

> How many **years** of retirement
> income will you need?
>
> How **much** income will you need each year?

Turn the page to learn more. Chapter 2 will unveil Blind Spot #1, and Chapter 3 will shine the light on Blind Spot #2.

Blind Spot #1
The Third Decade

So what are the blind spots that keep you from choosing the best withdrawal strategy for retirement? What don't you know that could keep you from plunging straight off the retirement mountain?

To see if you have Blind Spot #1, let's look at how you answer this question:

"How many years of retirement income will you need?"

25

How many years of retirement income will you need?

Well, it depends upon two things: It depends on the age that you retire and the age that you die.

So, let's start with the easy one — the age that you retire.

Fact#1: Average Retirement Age: 62 Years

Yes, a recent study found that the average retirement age was 62.[1] Seems young, doesn't it? But when you consider that you can choose to begin receiving your (discounted) Social Security checks at age 62, there's really no mystery here. The average retirement age in America will probably always match the first year we're eligible to begin receiving Social Security. If the age at which we receive benefits increases, the average retirement age will most likely follow suit.

Now, let's move on to the other variable in the question "How many years of retirement income will you need?" In most cases, you have control over when you retire, but when you die? Well, not so much.

How do you begin to figure out how many years you'll be on the planet, taking an income from your retirement savings? At what age do you think you're going to die? What is your own personal life expectancy?

Here is our first major challenge in creating a withdrawal strategy for never beginning to run out of money in retirement. You can't definitively calculate how many years your lifetime will be. It's a high-stakes guessing game. But nevertheless, we need some sort of an answer, so let's look at the facts.

Fact#2: Joint Life Expectancy of a married, non-smoking couple, both age 62: 92 years

If you're half of a couple that doesn't smoke and you're both 62 years old, it's likely that one of you will be alive at age 92.[2] Since 92 is the average, it's also likely that one of you will live *beyond* age 92. Having strong financial resources and access to progressive healthcare increases the odds that you'll someday be part of the over-92 crowd. But let's stick with averages for now and start calculating.

Okay, are you sitting down? It's time to do the math for "Retirement in the 21st Century":

$$92 - 62 = 30 \text{ years}$$

If you retire at 62, you're going to be retired for 30 years…30 YEARS!

This means you're going to need an income for 30 years. An income challenge like this is going to require one heck of a withdrawal strategy.

Blind Spot #1 is not seeing this fact:
You will need 30 years of income for retirement.

Don't worry. If you find these numbers hard to believe, you're in good company. Many of my focus group attendees were stunned by this news too. Seeing their wide-eyed stares when I revealed these numbers confirmed my hunch that the majority of retirees share Blind Spot #1. Most of today's retirees fail to plan for a 30-year retirement.

Insights from a Focus Group
To what age do you expect to live?

I included this question in a written survey I gave to each participant prior to our group discussion. Once the group was comfortable talking about their personal retirement experiences, I brought up this question. I told them I wasn't necessarily interested in the number they had written down, but what thought process they used to answer the question.

Almost every person in the room came to their answer in the same way. They considered how long their parents lived, or are living, and then added a few years for good behavior.

Maybe you did the same.

Most people tend to use their parents' ages as a guide when they're trying to determine how long they are likely to live. In real life, we don't consult the government's national life expectancy tables to plan our lives. We aren't average, so why should our life expectancy be average? After all, don't some people have longevity in their family history while others don't? Don't women tend to live longer than men?

Adding a few years to your parents' ages might seem logical, but it could be the biggest planning mistake you ever make. Basing your own life expectancy on the lifespan of the previous generation has never been more unreliable than it is for those of us born in the 20th century. To fully appreciate this, let's take a quick look at the past.

A Lesson from History

At the peak of the Roman Empire, sometime around A.D. 100, the average person could expect to live for about 28 years.[3] About 1700 years later (1800), Average Jane and Average Joe lived to the ripe old age of 35.[4] Over the course of those 1700 years, each generation lived only a few months longer than the previous generation lived. Back then, it was pretty safe to assume you'd live about as long as your parents had lived.

Then something dramatic happened. During the 19th century (1800 to 1900), the life expectancy for the average American lengthened by 12 years. People weren't living just a few *months* longer than the previous generation, they were living a few *years* longer. A significant achievement, but probably not widely noticed.

That brings us to the years 1900 to 2000. Of all the significant happenings of the 20th century, one that's often overlooked is the exponential lengthening of the American lifespan. During these 100 years, Americans' life expectancy lengthened by 30 years.[5]

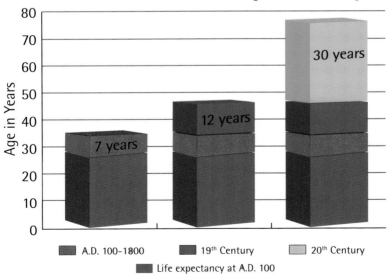

Growth in Life Expectancy

Age in Years

- A.D. 100-1800
- 19th Century
- 20th Century
- Life expectancy at A.D. 100

Let me say that again — a 30 years' gain in life expectancy over just 100 years. It turns out we who are nearing retirement age aren't living just a few years longer than our parents; we are living close to a full decade longer than our parents' generation.

Now, consider the fact that these government life expectancy tables are "lagging statistics." In other words, they're based on recent history and don't necessarily reflect what will happen to you in the future. There's a high likelihood that you will live *more* than 10 years beyond what your parents lived.

Do you know the average lifespan of a cow?

The law of averages says that a cow on a well-kept dairy farm will live about 20-25 years. But Big Bertha, born on St. Patrick's Day, 1944, obviously didn't consult the life expectancy tables. She lived almost 49 years, just missing the big barn bash that Farmer O'Leary had planned for her birthday. Big Bertha holds the record as the world's oldest cow.

Welcome to the 21st Century

I recently attended an industry conference with 120 of the best financial advisors in the country. We were there to participate in a workshop hosted by Nick Murray, one of our industry's most respected and knowledgeable writers/speakers. The discussion turned to retirement income planning. At one point, Nick posed a simple question to the room:

"Show of hands: How many of you have known a 90-year-old couple?"

Half of the hands went up.

So, what's going on here? Are we living longer because our genes went through some amazing evolution during the last two centuries? Of course not. We're living longer because we have more knowledge about nutrition and greater access to an ever improving healthcare system.

With each passing year, our life expectancy becomes less about genetics and more about rapidly advancing healthcare. Using the age of your parents as a guide is no longer the best way to estimate how long you are likely to live.

So why are our expectations still stuck in the 1800s? Why do so many of us think we'll live only a few years longer than our parents lived?

Because we have a blind spot! This blind spot leads us to plan for 20, not 30, years of retirement. And planning for 20 years of retirement — but living 30 years — is the easiest way to run out of money in your golden years. This is one of the things that will cause a fiscally responsible person to walk right off the cliff. And once you're off the cliff? Well, by the time you realize your error, it's too late to fix it.

A CLIENT STORY
The Trip of a Lifetime

Jim and Dorothy were inspired by the idea of retirement. After working for 40 years, they were going to take advantage of their good health and travel as much as possible while they still could. "Nobody is promised tomorrow," Jim was fond of saying. Dorothy adopted the same philosophy, and travel they did.

Their first 15 years of retirement took them to every continent, some more than once. They loved every minute. Whether because of the travel or in spite of it, both Jim and Dorothy were hailed by their doctors as "pictures of health" as they neared their 80th birthdays. There was only one problem. While their physical health was outstanding, their financial health was not.

"We didn't expect to live much past 80, so we spent like we wouldn't," Jim says now. "It was a great plan, we just lived too dang long. We really don't have much savings left. Soon we will be living only on our social security checks. I don't know how we are going to get by. I wish we had done things differently."

Summary

The first question you need to answer to choose an effective withdrawal strategy for retirement is this: *How many years of retirement income will you need?* Unfortunately, most of today's retirees fail to see that they need to plan for a 30-year retirement. This is Blind Spot #1.

This is not your parents' retirement. We're part of an unprecedented era in America's history — the first generation that can expect to be retired for 30 years. No other generation before us has done this, so there's no model for doing do it correctly. *We* must create the model. And because there are no do-overs, you have to get it right the first time.

Getting it right means choosing a withdrawal strategy that will provide you with an income for 30 years. This is the first criteria you'll use to evaluate whether or not your withdrawal strategy has what it takes to keep you on the retirement mountain, where you'll never begin running out of money.

Don't let a blind spot make you choose the wrong withdrawal strategy, or retire before you are financially prepared. Don't wait for the day you suddenly realize you're living longer than you expected — it's too late to correct the problem then.

Instead, start with the expectation that you will be retired for a *long* time — 30 years. Doing so will put you well on your way to creating a successful withdrawal strategy.

One blind spot down, one to go.

Next up: We need to figure out just how much those 30 years of retirement are going to actually cost you. It's time to answer our second question: *How much income will you need each year?*

Blind Spot #2:
The Double Whammy

Remember, our goal is to never begin running out of money in retirement. Now that you're aware of Blind Spot #1, you understand that to stay safely on the retirement mountain, you must plan to take an income from your retirement savings for 30 years. But that's just the first part of choosing the best withdrawal strategy for retirement.

" How **much** income will you **need** each year? "

Let's review the two questions that lay the foundation for creating an effective withdrawal strategy for retirement:

> How many **years** of retirement
> income will you need?
>
> How **much** income will you need each year?

It's time to look closely at the second question. In the process, we'll expose Blind Spot #2.

How much income will you need each year?

We're talking about creating a budget here. But how do you figure out what your annual living costs will be over the course of a 30-year retirement? We know that things will cost more in the future, but how much more? What will things cost in Year 15 of your retirement? How about in Year 23?

Here is our second major challenge in creating a withdrawal strategy for never beginning to run out of money in retirement. We need a method for determining what our annual living costs will be for a 30-year retirement. And we can't do that until we address Blind Spot #2.

What were you doing 30 years ago today?

Think back 30 years. Do you remember the name of your favorite rock group or your favorite restaurant? What kind of car did you own...and how much did you pay for it? Do you remember how 30 years ago, $100,000 was a small fortune?

What happened between then and now? Well, for starters, you became the older person you never imagined you'd be. The aging process is so gradual that you were probably surprised, like most of us, when you discovered your hair turning gray or your body shifting in odd new ways. When you turned 40, you didn't feel a day over 35. Next thing you knew, you were 50 years old, but felt like you were 40. Sixty? Well, who ever thought you'd get *there*?

And while we were all gradually changing over the course of the last 30 years, did you notice what was happening to prices? That's right — they were gradually, but steadily rising.

Most likely, you didn't pay much attention as the cost of things went up and up, year after year. But remember that car that you owned 30 years ago? What would a car of the same quality cost you today?

Rising costs are a simple fact of life. Economists call this upward movement of prices "inflation." Inflation has both positive and negative consequences. Sure, it's responsible for things costing more

Okay, time for "Popular Bands of the 60s and 70s" trivia!

What American singing group was made up of six siblings and their mother? Clue: The band is known for "Hair" and inspired the hit TV series *The Partridge Family.* Give up?

It was the Cowsills...of course! And they milked their name for all it was worth by doing commercials for the American Dairy Association too.

every year, but it's also the reason that employers increase salaries for their employees. Inflation is like a treadmill, and there's no way to step off of it. Fortunately, your increasing pay at work gives you the momentum to keep up with inflation.

But what happens when you stop working? What happens when you have a set amount of money (your retirement savings) that has to last you the rest of your life? Do costs stop rising for you then? Of course not. So how are you going to keep up with inflation?

Well, that's where your plan for taking an income from your retirement savings — your withdrawal strategy — comes in. The W/D strategy you choose will determine whether or not you can keep up with rising living costs.

You need to know in advance just how much income you'll need in the future. You need to consider rising costs — resulting from inflation — to figure out how much income you'll need for each of your 30 years of retirement.

Unfortunately, many retirees don't even *see* the enormous effect that inflation has on their retirement. This is Blind Spot #2. This too can easily cause you to choose the wrong withdrawal strategy and unknowingly walk right off the cliff. Like Blind Spot #1, Blind Spot #2 keeps you from realizing your mistake until it's too late to fix it. So by the time you figure out how much more the things you need are costing you every year of your retirement, you won't be able to avoid the cliff's edge — beginning to run out of money.

Blind Spot #2 is not seeing this fact:

Inflation is the biggest predictable challenge of a 30-year retirement.

Inflation is *the* biggest predictable challenge of a 30-year retirement. Yet this issue rarely gets the attention it deserves.

Personally, I blame the financial planning industry. We just don't do a very good job of helping you understand and deal with the impact of inflation on your retirement. We tell you that when you're 80 years old, a loaf of bread will cost $6.40 and a gallon of milk will cost $8.59, but that's not particularly helpful. I don't know about you, but I can't relate to this information in a way that makes me fully appreciate how rising costs affect everything else in my life. If you're like me, your first reaction to this information is "Heck, I'll just eat less bread" or "No problem, I'm lactose-intolerant."

Insights from a Focus Group

During our focus group discussions, I asked participants the following question.

What do you consider the three biggest risks to your retirement savings?

Here are their top five responses:

1. Health/Medical expenses
2. Government/Taxes
3. Terrorism
4. Market Volatility
5. Kids need money

Only one person mentioned inflation. Remember, all of these attendees are already retired — some have been for more than a decade— and they still didn't see the biggest predictable risk to their savings and in turn, their livelihoods. That's what I call a blind spot!

Have you considered the role inflation will play in your financial future?

Sometimes financial planners produce complicated spreadsheets to tell you what your living expenses are likely to be, each and every year, for the rest of your life. And I'll admit I've done that. But I find that most people don't really believe these numbers...at least not to the extent that they should.

So don't blame yourself for not immediately knowing how much things will cost in Year 15 or Year 23 of your retirement. But don't allow yourself to fall into the trap of thinking this isn't important or that you can just figure things out when you get there.

My industry insists on making it much more complicated than it needs to be. There actually is a simple way to figure out what your annual living costs will be over the course of a 30-year retirement.

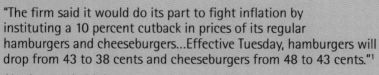

Would you like fries with that?

Here's a "rising costs" reality check from the *AP Newswire* (August 20, 1979) with a stunning announcement from the McDonald's Corporation:

"The firm said it would do its part to fight inflation by instituting a 10 percent cutback in prices of its regular hamburgers and cheeseburgers...Effective Tuesday, hamburgers will drop from 43 to 38 cents and cheeseburgers from 48 to 43 cents."[1]

Ah, the good old days...

A Simpler Approach

There are no loaves of bread, no gallons of milk, and no complex computer calculations required. All you need to know to determine how much money you will need in Year 15 or Year 23 of your retirement is this: a budget for the first year of your retirement. With that, the rest is simple.

If you're not the type of person that likes to create a budget, let alone live by it, I understand — I'm not either. But if ever there was a time that you should have a budget, it's your first year of retirement.

Think about it: This is the first year that you're living off a finite amount of money — your retirement savings. I urge you to get started on the right foot. A budget is the first step in making sure that you never begin running out of money.

Quick advice on creating a budget

The world doesn't need another budget tool...a quick internet search for a "budget worksheet" will provide you with many resources to assist you with this process. But let me add my own advice here, from someone who has helped a lot of people create a lot of budgets. Don't rely on just your memory when creating your budget. Use your actual financial statements.

People tend to underestimate their real expenses by 20% or more when trying to create a budget without the aid of their actual spending history. Many expenses are easily overlooked; things like subscriptions, taxes, insurance premiums, charitable gifts, even cheeseburgers and milkshakes. Using your checking, savings and credit card statements is the only way to get a true and accurate picture of how much money you spend each year.

Once you've created your first-year budget, calculate how much your retirement is going to cost by multiplying this annual budget figure by 3.37% (see "The U.S. Inflation Rate" on next page) and then compounding that amount each year for the next 30 years.

Wait a minute! Didn't I say this was going to be simple?

I did. So feel free to ignore all that multiplying and compounding stuff.

The U.S. Inflation Rate

The inflation rate varies considerably over time, depending on a variety of economic conditions.

3.37% is the average annual rate of inflation for the U.S economy since 1913.[2] During this period of time, our nation has experienced a lot: high inflation and low inflation; stock market booms and stock market busts; a presidential impeachment and a presidential assassination; multiple wars; more than one energy crisis; and perpetual threats of a global health epidemic.

This time span represents a good enough sample of economic history to give us a reliable rate of inflation for retirement planning purposes.

Doing the Math

We can simplify things by dividing your 30-year retirement into three segments — the three decades. Now, instead of trying to figure out what each and every year of retirement will cost, let's just figure out what each of the three decades will cost. Instead of needing 30 separate calculations, we need only three.

This is so straightforward, there's no spreadsheet required. In fact, don't even worry about pulling out your calculator — I've already done the work for you. All *you* need to do is remember your annual living cost from your first-year budget.

I applied the historical average inflation rate, compounded it year over year, carried the remainder, and rounded the numbers to eliminate fractions. The result? An easy-as-cow-pie formula for determining what each one of your three decades of retirement will cost:

Decade 1: Annual Living Costs = First Year Budget x 1

During the first decade of retirement, you can realistically expect your living costs each year to be just about the same as they were during your first year of retirement. In other words, to determine how much income you'll need each year for the first ten years of your retirement, multiply your first-year annual budget by one. And, simple as it seems, don't forget that you'll spend this much every year for 10 years.

Sure, your cable bill will gradually go up every year and you'll be spending a bit more at the supermarket, but for the most part, you won't notice the subtle effect of inflation during this first decade.

Decade 2: Annual Living Costs = First Year Budget x 1.5

The second decade of retirement is when you'll feel the unavoidable effects of inflation. Your budgeted lifestyle from Decade 1 will cost you 50% more in Decade 2. To find out what you'll be spending each year to maintain the same lifestyle you enjoyed during your first ten years of retirement, multiply your first-year annual budget by 1.5 for each of these ten years.

That 3.5% really adds up, doesn't it? Stop and take a deep breath... Now, let's keep going.

Decade 3: Annual Living Costs = First Year Budget x 2

Your third decade of retirement will cost twice as much as your first decade did. Let me say that again: *twice as much*...as in *double!* To put a real number to this bad-news equation, multiply your first-year annual budget by two. And again, you'll need ten times this amount to last the whole decade to never begin to run out of money during retirement.

Yikes, inflation is a real retirement killjoy, isn't it?

Allow this information about the three decades to really sink in. Your second decade of retirement is going to cost you half again as much as your first decade of retirement. More significantly, your third decade of retirement is going to cost you twice as much as the first decade. This third decade is the one that most retirees don't plan on being around for, but chances are, you will be.

How well prepared are your retirement savings to handle the financial challenge of the third decade? Well, that depends on which withdrawal strategy you choose at the beginning of your first decade of retirement.

Simply stated, in Decade 3, your retirement savings need to produce twice as much income as they did in Decade 1. If they won't, I'm sorry to say that you might be part of the herd that is headed off the cliff. Blind Spot #2 will have done you in.

But don't have a cow! Be glad that you're learning this information now. It would be much worse to have your living costs unexpectedly double after it's too late to do anything about it.

For you — a member of the first generation to live an average of 30 years in retirement — inflation is *the most serious* predictable risk to your future way of life. Inflation will wear away the purchasing power of your savings. Like aging, its effect is gradual, but unstoppable.

Your inflation rate is determined by what you buy

While inflation affects all of us, it doesn't affect us equally. Different age groups tend to experience different rates of inflation because they're buying different kinds of goods and services.

When we're younger, we tend to spend more on purchases that are considered *discretionary*. If an item is discretionary, we don't *have* to buy it if we think it's priced too high. For example, we all know that if we wait a couple years before we buy the latest hi-tech super-duper TV to hit the market, we'll probably get it for half of today's price. We have the *discretion* to wait until the price comes down.

But what about things that aren't discretionary — things we do *have* to buy — like food, electricity, gas for the car or healthcare? We don't have the luxury of waiting a couple years to see if the price goes down. And guess what? The price usually doesn't go down, it goes up. This simple fact impacts how much inflation we'll experience when we retire.

Why? Because most retirees spend the largest portion of their income on food, electricity, gasoline, and healthcare. There's just no way to avoid inflation when we retire. We must create a plan that enables us to keep up with it.

The Third Decade: A Double Whammy

As we learned in Chapter 2, most retirees don't expect to live for three decades after they stop working, so they don't plan to fund a third decade. And they certainly don't plan to fund a third decade that will cost twice as much as the first decade.

But like it or not, the longer we live, the more serious the challenge of inflation becomes to our finances and our lifestyles. The third decade is a double whammy!

Why do so many of the retirees I speak with not see these financial hazards? Why the blind spot when it comes to the impact of inflation?

Remember, a couple of generations ago people retired, and then typically died about five years later. Inflation was the last thing that retirees worried about; it just wasn't noticeable over that short period of time. Given that today's retirees are using their parents' experiences to project their own, it's easy to see why this is a blind spot for so many.

Insights from a Focus Group

After our discussion, I shared the Three Decade Multiplier Chalkboard with the group. The room went silent. After that moment, I'm not sure they heard anything I said for the rest of the meeting.

If you have a knot in your stomach after reading this chapter, you're not alone. But you have withdrawal strategy options that can make a difference.

The Calculator

Bob is a retired engineer and has a knack for numbers. He is the type of guy who could tell you how much his last restaurant tab was...to the penny. One day we got on the topic of inflation and Bob began to tell me the story of how much things cost when he was just starting out his career.

"I bought my first used car right after I graduated college in 1965. A decent new car at the time cost around $3,000, which was way beyond my budget. Heck they were only paying me $8,950 a year when I started. I eventually found a used Plymouth Fury for which I paid $175.

"When Sue and I got married a couple years later, we bought a three-bedroom house for $24,700 and wondered how we would ever be able to pay it off. That house today probably sells for 10 times as much. Heck, everything used to cost so much less. I remember writing to her when I was off at college and saving my nickels to buy stamps...that's how much they cost back in 1964.

"About the only thing that has gone down in price since I got out of college is the calculator. Funny story, we engineers were using slide rules until the late 60s. The company bought us our first handheld calculators in 1972. We called them The Bowmar Brain *after the Bowmar Company that made them. They cost the company $240 each. Imagine that."*

Summary

To choose an effective withdrawal strategy for retirement, after discovering how many years of retirement income you will need, you'll need the answer to this question: *How much income will you need each year?* Unfortunately, even if they know to ask this question, most retirees don't answer it correctly because they don't see the enormous effect that inflation has on their retirement. This is Blind Spot #2.

Rising costs are a fact of life, no matter how long you live. And the longer you live, the bigger a challenge they present. But let's put it in perspective. Humorist Kin Hubbard got it right when he said:

"So far I haven't heard of anybody who wants to stop living on account of the cost."

Nobody wants to outlive their money in retirement. And nobody wants to stop living because they ran out of money. So you must choose a withdrawal strategy that allows your retirement savings to keep up with the rising cost of living. This is the only way to never begin running out of money.

If your withdrawal strategy isn't designed to do this for you, you'll find yourself going off the mountain cliff at some point during your retirement. You'll begin running out of money. And once you do, you'll begin losing the quality of life that makes retirement great.

Next up: So far, you've learned that there are three steps for never beginning to run out of money in retirement:
1: Know your blind spots.
2: Choose a withdrawal strategy that adjusts for these blind spots.
3: Manage your withdrawal strategy appropriately.

Now that we've covered the first step and uncovered your blind spots, we'll move on to the second step: choosing a withdrawal strategy that adjusts for these blind spots.

Choose a Withdrawal Strategy that Adjusts for These Blind Spots

Part 2

We in the 21st century are living in unprecedented times. Your 21st century retirement calls for a 21st century withdrawal strategy for taking an income from your retirement savings. After reading Part 1, you're now well aware of your blind spots. You now know that you'll need a withdrawal strategy that will provide an income for three decades and keep up with rising living costs (inflation) during the second and third decades.

You can see that "never running out of money" in retirement just isn't good enough. Living a financially successful retirement is about more than not outliving your money. It's about always having enough money to enjoy the lifestyle you want and deserve. It means never *beginning* to run out of money.

Turn the page to learn more. Chapter 4 will tell you more about retiring in the 21st century, including what "beginning to run out of money" really means and how you'll know if or when that's happening. And in Chapters 5, 6, and 7, we'll look at the three most common withdrawal strategies retirees use to take an income from their retirement savings.

Requirements of a 21ˢᵗ Century Withdrawal Strategy

Chapter

" A 21ˢᵗ Century **retirement** requires a 21ˢᵗ Century withdrawal **strategy.** "

Holy Cow!

It's 3:00 a.m. — you're sound asleep and then suddenly you're not. Your eyes are wide open and you're staring at the ceiling with a series of thoughts running through your mind:

"I don't have to go to work tomorrow, I don't have to get up early, I don't have to do anything tomorrow...wait...I don't have anything to do tomorrow, what should I do tomorrow, I can't believe I'm finally retired, holy cow, I'm retired, I don't have to work for a living, I can live off my retirement savings...wait...can I live off my savings, do I have enough money to last me the rest of my life, I hope I have enough money to last me the rest of my life, what if I live longer than I thought or get sick, how am I going to have enough money to last the rest of my life, I'm not going to have enough money to last, I shouldn't have retired, I should have worked a couple more years just to be sure, can I go back to work, I can't go back to work, how am I going to do this, I need to call my advisor first thing in morning."

Welcome to the first Holy Cow Moment of your retirement.

Retirement is a major life change and it takes time to adjust. The Holy Cow Moment (HCM) is a common emotional experience that usually happens sometime during the first month of retirement. I know this is true because I have gotten plenty of these early morning calls from recent retirees.

And do I reassure these nice, sleep-deprived folks that their money will not run out in retirement? Of course, because I've already helped them choose the right withdrawal strategy for their retirement savings. They just needed to be reminded of it.

What's so "holy" about a cow?
Well, in India, the cow holds a sacred status. This animal is respected as the source of nurturing milk and revered as a symbol of life and abundance. The cow is also connected to the Hindu belief in reincarnation. In India, cows freely roam city streets, causing drivers to regularly exclaim, "Holy Cow! That was a close one!"

Choosing a 21st Century Withdrawal Strategy

As we've discussed, these are unprecedented times. Your 21st century retirement calls for a 21st century withdrawal strategy for taking an income from your retirement savings. Since you're now well aware of your blind spots, you know that you'll need a withdrawal strategy that will provide an income for three decades *and* keep up with rising living costs (inflation) during the second and third decades.

We've set the bar high. We've said that "never running out of money" in retirement just isn't good enough. Living a financially successful retirement is about more than not outliving your money. It's about always having enough money to enjoy the lifestyle you want and deserve. It means never *beginning* to run out of money.

What does "beginning to run out of money" really mean? And how will you know if or when that's happening?

Remember, your retirement savings may include investments, retirement accounts, savings accounts, or brokerage accounts that you plan to use to create an income in retirement. Most people look at the value of these savings to answer these questions. If the value has gone up, they think, "No problem." If it has gone down, they think, "Uh oh, I'm beginning to run out of money."

This may or may not be true, and in Chapter 10 we'll refine our answer. For now, let's keep things simple.

If you're taking an income that keeps up with the rising cost of living and your nest egg is steadily declining *each and every year*, you can be sure that you've begun to run out of money. But if you're taking an income each year that keeps up with the rising cost of living and your nest egg is *not* decreasing in value, then you have *not* begun to run out of money. We can safely say that "never beginning to run out of money" means *maintaining* the value of your retirement savings over time.

Of course, maintaining the value of your retirement savings would be easy if you didn't need to use that money to live on. But come on, let's be real here. There's no doubt that taking a regular income — or regular withdrawals — from your nest egg creates a stress on your savings. It increases the likelihood that you might *begin* running out of money at some point during your retirement. Once that happens, there's a chance that you might just run out of money altogether. And that just won't do.

It's time to get serious about the importance of choosing a withdrawal strategy that keeps you safely on the retirement mountain...and not involuntarily diving off the cliff.

A withdrawal strategy for the 21st century needs to do three things:
1. Maintain the value of your retirement savings over time.
2. Provide an income for 30 years.
3. Provide an income that keeps up with rising living costs (inflation).

And here's the good news: There *is* a withdrawal strategy that delivers on all three counts. As you'll learn, it's actually easy to create a withdrawal strategy that lets you enjoy life on the mountain.

Even if you've chosen the right withdrawal strategy, let's be honest; you may still experience the Holy Cow Moment. That's understandable. But when I get a call from a client who has just had her first HCM, I review the three standards for evaluating a good withdrawal strategy and confidently remind her that she'll have enough money to last her lifetime.

And then I tell her to go back to bed.

The Wood-Burning Stove

At 88 years old, Helen is no longer lifting the heavy cinder blocks used to build one-room churches in the impoverished neighborhoods of Brazil, at least not physically. Spiritually? Well, that's another story altogether.

I first met Helen in 1997, soon after she had returned from one of these mission trips. She invited me to her home to see the pictures of her latest "Vacation Bible School", and it is an experience I will never forget. Every picture had a story. A story of people in need. A story of people helping people. A story of faith. Tears of joy streamed down her face as she recounted the people she met and experiences she had there.

Helen lives a modest lifestyle by choice (except for her shiny Cadillac). Financially, she isn't in need, never will be in need, and is living a life that is rewarded by that.

After one hip replacement and two knee replacements, Helen hasn't felt up to making the trip in the last few years; but she still stays connected and hears the stories from others of the lasting impact she made in that country 4,000 miles away.

At home she still tends her own garden, mows her own yard, and even carries in the wood to fuel the wood-burning stove she uses to heat her home. I've been next to that stove, and I can only imagine that the tremendous warmth I have felt from it is only a fraction of the warmth Helen carries in her heart from the difference she has made for others in this world.

Summary

Making sure that the quality of your lifestyle is never compromised means making sure you never begin to run out of money. The moment you realize that you're running out of money is the moment you've lost your financial stability.

A financially stable retirement is too important to leave to chance. You need a plan.

Your plan is a withdrawal strategy that addresses the blind spots that can cause you to go off the retirement mountain cliff. A successful withdrawal strategy for the 21st century must meet these objectives:

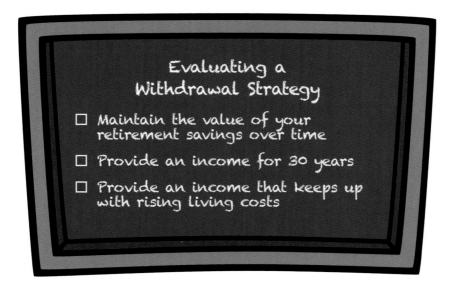

Evaluating a
Withdrawal Strategy

☐ Maintain the value of your retirement savings over time

☐ Provide an income for 30 years

☐ Provide an income that keeps up with rising living costs

If your withdrawal strategy fails to do any one of these, you may find yourself involuntarily cliff-diving. You will have officially begun to run out of money in retirement.

But the right withdrawal strategy — one that meets the three objectives — gives you the confidence that you'll be able to enjoy the retirement lifestyle you desire and deserve.

Next up: Over the next three chapters, we'll look at the three most common withdrawal strategies retirees use to take an income from their retirement savings. We'll be using the same example — a nest egg of $500,000 — to see what happens when you take an income from your retirement savings using each of the three strategies. These strategies each come with their own lifestyle implications, which we'll also discuss.

By the end of Part 2, I guarantee that you'll know exactly which withdrawal strategy really works. There's only *one* that adjusts for your blind spots. This is the only strategy that maintains the value of your retirement savings over time, provides an income that will last for 30 years and provides an income that keeps up with the rising living costs (inflation) of the second and third decades. This withdrawal strategy puts you on the right path...one that won't lead you off the cliff of your retirement mountain.

Withdrawal Strategy #1:
Spending Down

The Withdrawal Strategy: Spending Down

Keeping in mind that you're looking for a withdrawal strategy that keeps you on the retirement mountain (and not involuntarily diving off the cliff), take a look at this withdrawal strategy that combines a very simple plan and a very simple mindset. The Spend Down (SD) Strategy boils down to this financial objective:

> "I want to spend my last dollar on my last day."

The strategy's *fatal* flaw (pardon the pun) jumps out pretty quickly here: It's impossible to know when your "last day" will be. Will it be next Wednesday? How about Tuesday, June 8, 2038? Depending on your answer, the amount you'll be able to spend each day differs greatly.

This is a miserable way to manage your money. It's also a miserable way to live.

> " Hey, you **can't** take it with you. "

59

Not all retirees are blunt enough to say that they want to spend their last dollar on their last day. Sometimes I hear variations on the same short-sighted theme:

"Hey, you can't take it with you."

"I plan to live before I die."

"Finances have a way of working themselves out."

"I don't want to leave any money on the table."

"If I don't have kids, why leave an inheritance?"

"What, me worry?"

Doomed from the Start

Without even seeing the numbers, you know that, using the Spend Down Strategy, it won't be long before you begin running out of money.

But here's the sad part. Most people don't actively choose the SD Strategy for their retirement. They end up "spending down" because of poor planning — a direct result of their blind spots.

Let's first take a look at how a SD Strategy works financially, and then we'll talk about how it impacts a retiree's lifestyle.

The truth is out — cow tipping is a myth.
Cows may catch an occasional nap standing up, but they sleep lying down. That means that all those frat-boy stories about sneaking up on a standing, slumbering cow and pushing her right over — well, they're just bull. Weighing in at over half a ton, even a dozing Daisy just isn't going down!

The Numbers

A retiree starts with $500,000 in retirement savings from which he or she intends to create an income. Check out the math on how this SD Strategy works each year.

Retirement Savings: $500,000
Invested to Earn: 5%
Annual withdrawal: $40,000

The Spend Down Strategy

Year	Beginning Savings Value		Investment Earnings		Annual Withdrawal		Year End Savings Value
1	$500,000	+	$25,000	−	$40,000	=	$485,000
2	$485,000	+	$24,250	−	$40,000	=	$469,250
3	$469,250	+	$23,463	−	$40,000	=	$452,713
4	$452,713	+	$22,636	−	$40,000	=	$435,348

Wow. Talk about a short-sighted strategy! If this was your strategy, you'd clearly be taking more income than your retirement savings investments are able to generate. You'd be spending money faster than your investments can earn it.

For example, in Year 1, you take your desired withdrawal of $40,000, but your investments earned only $25,000. This leaves you with a smaller savings at the end of the year, which in turn will earn you less interest next year.

This effect is cumulative. With each passing year, the total value of your savings gets smaller, meaning that it earns *even less* interest. All the while, your spending stays the same. Take a look:

Spend Down Strategy

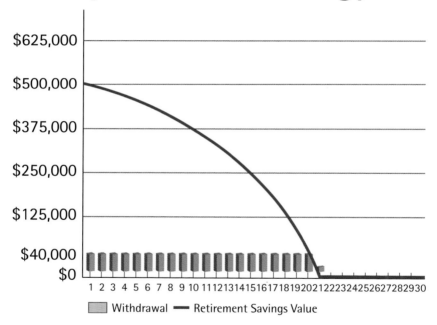

In this example, your steadily eroding retirement savings is completely *gone* by the 21st year of your retirement. Is that the year you were planning to die? If so, you succeeded in spending your last dollar on your last day. Congratulations.

And if not? *What, me worry?*

Please don't forget Blind Spot #1! You're likely to live for *three* decades in retirement, not two. What will that third decade be like if your savings are gone? For that matter, what will the first and second decades of the spend-down experience be like? And remember Blind Spot #2 — costs are rising, but your income isn't even beginning to keep pace with inflation.

> Blind spots cause retirees to choose
> a withdrawal strategy that sends
> them into a financial free-fall.

Let's talk about the lifestyle of a Spend Down retiree, in the hope that you'll *never* dive off the cliff's edge.

The Lifestyle Path: Straight Off the Cliff

The SD Strategy means choosing to take a plunge off the cliff in the very first year of retirement. The *very day* you begin to spend down your money faster than your investments can generate it, you have one foot off the cliff.

Most people probably know they're in trouble when they see the shrinking value of their retirement savings. Once they feel themselves beginning to go over the cliff, many grab for the nearest branch. This may mean going back to work or making immediate lifestyle changes. If they catch themselves early enough, some retirees do manage to pull themselves back from the edge. This is the point where do-it-yourself investors finally call an advisor. Good for them! With help, they may actually be able to adjust their investments and their spending accordingly.

Other retirees are voluntary cliff-divers. They just don't get the disastrous reality of the Spend Down Strategy and refuse to break their suicidal spending down habits. For them, going off the cliff becomes a slow-motion free-fall.

I need to get very serious for a minute here.

Imagine a life of guilt, worry, and fear. Every year, you get news that your financial situation is worse than it was the year before. Even if you tell yourself that everything will work out fine, down deep you know it won't. Little by little, you are losing everything you worked so hard to enjoy in your retirement years.

Cutting back on your expenses may slow your descent, but the truth is...you are still falling.

With every purchase you make, you know you're running out of money that much sooner. You feel guilty about every dollar you spend. Say, for example, that you decide to splurge on a Caribbean cruise for a milestone anniversary. How much do you think you will enjoy a trip you know you can't afford? Fear is your constant companion when you've gone off the cliff. There's just no escaping the fact that someday you're going to hit rock bottom. It's unavoidable; you'll be flat out of money.

Who will take care of you? What will happen to your house, your belongings, everything you worked for? What if you get sick?

And to make matters worse, other people in your life will be affected by your short-sightedness. Will your financial burdens fall to your children? To your siblings?

The closer you come to hitting the rocky ravine, the more life becomes about day-to-day survival. You're pinching pennies, trying to delay the inevitable. How does it feel knowing you have only enough money to last a few years?

This fall really takes its toll. Your self-worth, your sense of purpose, and your ability to make a difference are distant memories. To be brutally honest, the only difference you can make at this point is to keep from becoming a burden to others.

Depressing picture, isn't it? But that's exactly what the spending down descent is — depressing. It's a downward plunge that begins as soon as you start spending more money than your retirement savings can regularly earn. Whether you're 75 or 95 when you enter a spend down mode, the result's the same.

Why would anyone work for 30 to 40 years and then knowingly set themselves up for misery in their "golden years"?

Insights From A Focus Group
When I discussed the Spend Down Strategy with my focus groups, one of the participants had this comment:

"My kids have professional careers and are making more money than I ever did. They really don't need an inheritance from me. They've even told me to go enjoy what I worked so hard to save. Why isn't it right for me to say that it's not important to me to have any money left over?"

My response: "There is nothing wrong with saying that. This isn't a moral discussion at all. In fact, it isn't even about your kids. It's about *you*. It's about *your lifestyle* in retirement. Will it be one burdened by the idea of running out of money and possibly becoming a financial burden on your children, or one where you really feel able to do as your kids suggested and enjoy what you worked so hard for? You didn't work hard for money, you worked hard to enjoy the lifestyle you want before and after retirement, and the dignity that comes with that."

Is this true of you?

As expected, the Spend Down Strategy fails all three criteria for a successful 21st century withdrawal strategy.

Since it's specially designed to run out of money, the SD Strategy will never maintain the value of your savings. As for providing an income for a 30-year retirement...it doesn't even come close. And what about keeping up with rising living costs? No way. This strategy is too busy running out of money — it falls behind each and every year.

This withdrawal strategy results in a progressive deterioration of your lifestyle and the worry and mental anguish that comes with it.

Summary

You've now seen the ugly truth of voluntary cliff-diving.

The Spend Down Strategy is a withdrawal strategy that takes more income each year from your retirement savings than your investments are able to earn. It completely ignores both blind spots — it fails to provide you with an income for 30 years and it fails to keep up with inflation.

Because its damaging effects are cumulative, the SD Strategy comes with an unwritten guarantee that you'll run out of money sooner or later. In fact, you've begun to run out of money the very day you decide to spend down your retirement savings. That's the day you've chosen to go over the cliff.

Next up: I hope by now, you're willing to do whatever it takes to avoid the terrible path of the Spend Down Strategy. Once both feet go off the cliff, it's impossible to turn back. Avoiding this fate requires a better strategy — one that doesn't pick the year in which you'll run out of money. You need a strategy that ensures your savings will never run out.

In Chapter 6, we'll look at Strategy #2, which promises to do just that.

Withdrawal Strategy #2:
Living Off the Interest

The Withdrawal Strategy: Living Off the Interest

In order to stay safely on the retirement mountain, your goal is to never *begin* running out of money, right? When it comes to choosing a withdrawal strategy, we may want to say this in a slightly different way: Your goal in retirement is to *not* spend your principal. It follows that if your principal (which earns you interest) stays intact, you can never run out of money.

This is the reasoning behind the Living Off the Interest (LOI) Strategy. It's the strategy that many retirees are banking on when they tell me how they'd like to have their money invested. Typically, this is what I hear:

> " If I don't **spend** my principal, I can't run out of **money**. "

"I want to protect my principal and live off the interest."

"I don't want any investments that can lose money."

"If I can earn 5% interest, that'll be fine. Give me something stable."

"I want an income that's guaranteed not to change."

"Just keep the value of my savings the same; that way I'll be able to sleep at night."

These comments make sense...much more sense than those of the Spending Down crowd. The LOI Strategy gives retirees the confidence that they can successfully live off the interest from their retirement savings. The strategy is simple. And it's powerful too, because it promises to keep your savings intact and help you sleep well at night.

Now, let's take a closer look at this mathematical mastermind of a strategy.

The Numbers

Like our Spend Down Strategy example, a retiree starts with $500,000 in retirement savings, from which he or she intends to create an income. Unlike our SD example, our retiree will be spending $25,000 instead of $40,000 each year. The premise of the LOI Strategy is that you spend only what you earn — not more. Yes, it means less money each year, but the payoff is worth it.

Let's take a look:

Retirement Savings: $500,000
Invested to Earn: 5%
Annual withdrawal: ~~$40,000~~ $25,000

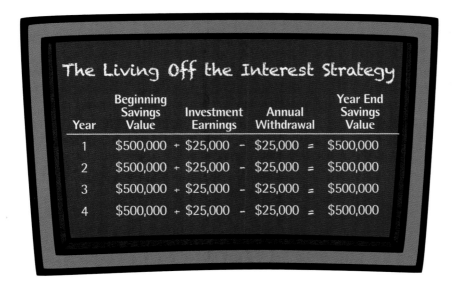

The Living Off the Interest Strategy

Year	Beginning Savings Value		Investment Earnings		Annual Withdrawal		Year End Savings Value
1	$500,000	+	$25,000	−	$25,000	=	$500,000
2	$500,000	+	$25,000	−	$25,000	=	$500,000
3	$500,000	+	$25,000	−	$25,000	=	$500,000
4	$500,000	+	$25,000	−	$25,000	=	$500,000

The LOI Strategy creates an income that's very predictable…and see how you never run out of money? Heck, you never even touch your principal. At the end of each year, the value of your savings is always the same…always there, working away, earning interest for you. Genius! And all it takes is the discipline to spend only what you earn. Do that and you've mastered the LOI Strategy.

This is such a big improvement over the Spend Down Strategy, where spending more than you earned resulted in an ever-shrinking nest egg. The payoff, seen in the graph "*Comparing Nest Egg Values,*" speaks for itself:

Comparing Nest Egg Values

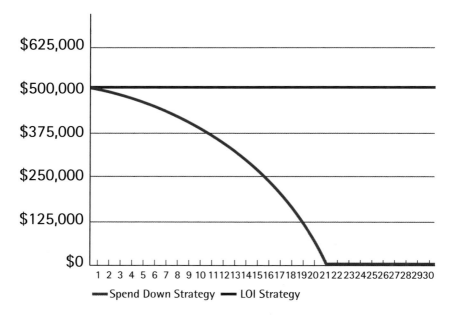

Spend Down Strategy — LOI Strategy

So, this shows that the LOI Strategy gives you a way to manage your retirement savings so that you never begin running out of money.

Or does it?

Graphs can be deceiving...and so can the LOI Strategy. Take a minute and see if you can figure out what's wrong with this strategy. Hint: Blind Spot #2: The Double Whammy caused by inflation.

We know that rising costs are the biggest challenge of a three-decade retirement. Inflation means that your third decade will cost *twice* as much as your first.

Wow, that's a game-changer. Let's apply this reality to the income generated by the LOI Strategy:

LOI Strategy
Income Falls Short

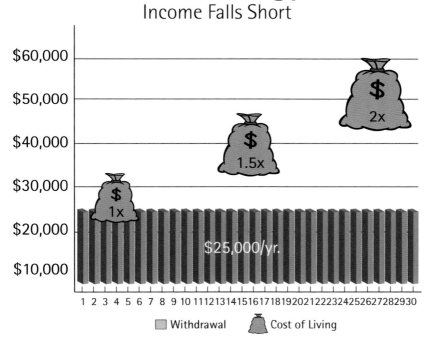

Losing Ground

Choosing this strategy means you'll be steadily losing ground during the second and third decades of your retirement.

As good as this strategy looks on paper (or chalkboard), it ignores the impact of inflation. It's completely removed from the reality of three decades of rising living costs. Sure, it gives you a predictable income that's *guaranteed never to change*, but you're living in a world where costs are *guaranteed to rise*!

You'll be okay for the first decade. But in Decade 2, this strategy will give you one dollar to pay for things that now cost $1.50.

You'll probably react by cutting back — you won't buy as much, won't do as much in that second decade. Maybe you'll decide that since you're getting older, you don't really care about traveling anyway. You'll make it work somehow, you tell yourself. And this may be possible…but is it what you want?

Let's say that you somehow manage to cut back your lifestyle and keep your retirement savings principal protected during Decade 2. But what does Decade 3 hold in store for you?

Your strategy will give you one dollar to pay for things that now cost $2.00. You've already done all the cutting back you can do. I've heard of "senior citizen discounts," but none that give you a 50% discount…on everything!

That leaves you only one option: You'll have to begin spending your principal, and you'll be spending it at a frightening rate. Remember, your goal in retirement is to *not* spend your principal. Once you do, you're beginning to run out of money.

To make matters worse, we're assuming that you'll have only your normal living expenses, without any added health or medication costs. Considering how old you'll be at this point, does this seem realistic to you?

The Lifestyle Path: Beware of Erosion

The Living Off the Interest Strategy doesn't lead you straight off the cliff; its path winds its way along the edge of the cliff.

Your first decade with the LOI Strategy fools you into thinking you've made a smart choice about your money. The path looks safe and you're doing fine, at least at first.

But your footing on this retirement mountain path eventually gets tricky — stones begin to shift underfoot. You've got to watch your step. Your budget gets a tiny bit tighter each year. Somehow you manage, but you find yourself worrying about the future. Erosion is beginning to wear down your retirement mountain.

During the second decade, you realize that your costs that have been rising aren't going to stop rising. The strategy that's giving you an income guaranteed never to change means that your income is guaranteed to fall behind your expenses.

By the third decade, your retirement mountain is crumbling more with every step you take. You're getting more and more nervous — this path is way too close to the cliff for comfort. The ground is so unstable that you realize you could go over the cliff at any time. You're living on the edge.

We could rename this strategy The Penny-Pincher Plan. Your lifestyle is all about cutting back and doing without — and it's not just the things you want, it's the things you need too. You lose sleep worrying about how you'll pay for the furnace that breaks down, the roof that's leaking, or the heart medications that your spouse depends on.

You eventually face the fact that you're going to have to begin spending your principal. And you know what that means…you're officially in spend down mode.

At this point, there's no turning back. You've just gone over the cliff.

A Generation of Cliff-Divers

As a retirement income planning professional, here's what concerns me most: People think that the LOI Strategy actually works. Not all people, of course, but enough of them to potentially create the largest welfare generation in our country's history. A generation of involuntary cliff-divers.

Remember that research study that projected half of baby boomers will run out of money in their retirements?[1] Well, in many cases, it's not only that baby boomers didn't save enough; but also the fact that so many of them are adopting an LOI Strategy. And it's all because of their blind spots.

> Blind spots cause retirees to choose a withdrawal strategy that sends them into a financial free-fall.

This generation of cliff-divers will be made up of formerly middle-class folks who carefully saved for retirement, and then chose a dangerous financial strategy that they thought was perfectly safe. I consider it my personal mission to sound a loud and steady warning about the LOI Strategy. I want to remove peoples' blind spots so that they can see this strategy for what it really is — a lifestyle/nest egg killer.

Cows' herding instinct

Cows are, by nature, social animals. They like the safety and solidarity of hangin' with the herd, which can number up to 300 animals. Cows recognize and respond to each other, forming strong bonds with their families and preferred herd members. As part of a herd, cows tend to act together, but not in a planned, coordinated effort. Bovine buddies simply imitate the behaviors of others in their group...even when it means walking off a cliff.

Seeing this, you may think be thinking, "Well, two out of three ain't bad."

In this case, two out of three is *very* bad. The LOI Strategy is designed to maintain the value of your retirement savings and provide an income for 30 years. Because it achieves these first two objectives so easily, it has the power to seduce you into thinking you're living a financially successful retirement.

But the strategy simply can't keep up with rising living costs. It's not designed to. Former financial advisor and speaker Nick Murray said it best when he described such a plan as "a fixed income investment strategy in a rising cost world."[2]

The "Perfect" Retirement

Ed and Ruby never thought money would be a problem. They had retired at the "perfect time."

The year was 1994. The Federal Reserve had just announced the seventh interest rate increase in the last 12 months to try to slow the overheating economy. For them, this meant that CD rates were almost 3% higher than just one year before. What luck!

Ed and Ruby saw a newspaper ad from their local bank offering a 10-year CD paying 8% interest. After working out their retirement budget, they determined that they would be able to live on the interest from the CD alone, and never need to spend their principal.

As it turned out, over the term of the CD, the 8% annual interest income was adequate. Ed and Ruby had noticed the budget seemed to be getting a little tighter during the last couple of years, but they managed. They no longer lavished the grandchildren with numerous Christmas presents, and had skipped a couple of church trips; but both agreed they still felt reasonably comfortable in their retirement. Then came 2004.

Ed and Ruby received a notice in their mailbox from their bank. Their 10-year 8% CD was about to mature. In addition to this information, the bank notice also included an offer to renew their CD for another 10-year term at the now current available rate. That rate: 4%.

Their income was about to be cut in half. What once seemed like a perfect plan became a financial hardship they had never dreamed could happen. Yes, they still had their social security and a "rainy day" fund, but their main source of income was the interest from this CD. They couldn't cut back enough; they would be forced to spend their principal. They were beginning to run out of money.

Summary

The Living Off the Interest Strategy gives retirees the confidence that they can successfully live off the interest from their retirement savings and keep their saved principal intact. This withdrawal strategy is appealing because of its simplicity and its promise to provide you with an income for the rest of your life.

But the LOI Strategy fails because it ignores Blind Spot #2 — the impact of inflation. Rising costs mean that your third decade will cost twice as much as your first. With this strategy, throughout your retirement years, your income remains the same while your cost of living goes up.

Insights from a Focus Group

I noticed a trend as I discussed the Living Off the Interest Strategy with my focus groups, a phenomenon I call "The Generational Mindset of the LOI Strategy."

As one participant put it, "Wow, I actually thought this was the way to do it. My parents grew up in the depression and had always told me to put my money in the bank where it was guaranteed, safe, and paying me some interest.

"In fact most of my friends are doing it this way as well. I hadn't thought of it like you have shown us here. This strategy isn't really safe at all. Each year that goes by, I'm falling behind.

"It worked for my parents because they didn't need it to last that long. After seeing this 30 year graph, it's easy to see that this isn't going to work for me."

My response: "I couldn't have said it better myself. I'm glad you came today."

Have you been approaching your retirement with this particular generational mindset?

You may think you're on a safe path with the LOI Strategy, but from the very first year of your retirement, your financial stability is eroding right under your feet. By the time you realize this — usually during the second decade — it's too late to turn back. You're faced with the choice of constantly cutting back your lifestyle, or worse, spending your principal and going into Spend Down mode.

Next up: Becoming aware of the LOI mistake is just the first step. Now, you need a strategy that actually works — one that provides you with a *rising* income throughout your retirement. Happily, just such a strategy really does exist. I give you my word.

Withdrawal Strategy #3:
Rising Income

By now, you may be feeling overwhelmed by the retirement income challenge. The three-decade retirement dilemma, coupled with the rising costs of inflation...holy cow. How does *anyone* manage to avoid plunging off the cliff?

Let's go back and review why the first two withdrawal strategies didn't work:

Spend Down Strategy – Spending more than you earn each year means your retirement nest egg is always shrinking. You never stand a chance with this one. You'll be running out of money in retirement and be miserable the whole time.

Living Off the Interest Strategy – Spending only what you earn is a successful way to maintain the value of your retirement nest egg, but your income won't keep up with your rising living costs. Inflation will make you poor, forcing you to drastically curb your lifestyle, or worse, adopt the Spend Down Strategy.

> " When you spend **less** than you **earn** something **magical** happens. "

Both plans fail because of how much you're spending. So…what if, during your retirement years, you *spend less than you earn*?

Well, that's when something magical happens. You have money left over…and that money begins working for you. Your money begins compounding. Ben Franklin was a huge fan of compounding. Here's what he said:

> "Compound interest is the eighth wonder of the world."

I happen to agree with Ben. But what he didn't mention is that the mighty power of compounding works both *for you* and *against you*.

We've said that the LOI Strategy fails because inflation is constantly working against you. The fixed income that the LOI Strategy creates buys you less and less as time goes on, making you poorer each and every year.

But inflation in and of itself isn't the culprit. It's the *compounding* of inflation that's Public Enemy #1. There's no way that a fixed income can keep up with those gradual cost increases year after year, one piled on top of the other.

During previous generations, when the average retirement lasted about 10 years, these rising costs really weren't an issue. Heck, even in 20 years of retirement, you could pinch pennies and find a way to make it work. In a 30-year retirement, it's a different story — compounding inflation is going to get you.

When you choose the LOI strategy, you're like a cow standing idle in the middle of a stampede — you're likely to get trampled. But by joining the rush, you can take advantage of the power of compounding to get ahead. It's a matter of choosing a plan that makes compounding work *for* you.

How do you do that? Simply spend less than you earn — or earn more than you spend, which ever makes more sense to you — and reinvest what's left over. This is the foundation of the Rising Income Strategy.

The Withdrawal Strategy: Rising Income

The Rising Income (RI) Strategy is based upon one simple concept: If you want to never begin running out of money, you need to *grow* your nest egg during retirement.

Think about it. A larger retirement nest egg has the ability to generate larger earnings. As the value of your nest egg is rising, so is your income. Behold...the Rising Income Strategy.

The RI Strategy involves four practices that are different than the ones we've seen in the Spend Down and Living Off the Interest Strategies:

■ First, you're going to **spend less than you earn**. Instead of taking a fixed $40,000/year withdrawal as in the SD Strategy, or a 5% withdrawal as in the LOI Strategy, in your first year of retirement you'll take a 4% withdrawal. This percentage is, in general, what I'd recommend for a 62-year-old retiree. The percentage withdrawal that's right for you may be different, based on variables like your age and the value of your savings. We'll discuss this in more detail in Part 3.

- Second, you'll **invest to earn more.** You'll be investing your retirement savings in a way that lets it earn a higher return over your three-decade retirement. Instead of owning investments that pay only a fixed income, you'll invest in a portfolio that provides both growth and income. This is essential for creating an income *and* keeping up with inflation. For our purposes, let's use the example of a steady 7.5% return on your investments. (We'll discuss how this works in the real world in the next chapter.)

- Third, you're going to **reinvest your leftover earnings.** If you're spending less than you earn, you're going to have money left over. You'll be reinvesting this back into your retirement savings. This is how you'll get compounding working *for* you.

- Fourth, you'll **give yourself a pay raise each year.** This strategy is called the Rising Income Strategy for a good reason. To keep up with rising living costs, you'll pay yourself a rising income over your retirement years. To win out over that "Double Whammy" you learned was Blind Spot #2, your raise should mirror inflation. And as I said in Chapter 3, inflation has averaged 3.37%; so to err on the conservative side and keep things simple, you will give yourself a pay raise of 3.5 % each year. (Well, there will likely be at least a few exceptions, but we'll get to that in Part 3.)

The Numbers

Just as in our previous examples, a retiree starts with $500,000 in retirement savings, from which he or she intends to create an income. Applying the new criteria, let's take a look at the numbers of the Rising Income Strategy:

> Retirement Savings: $500,000
> Invested to Earn: 7.5%
> First Year Withdrawal: $20,000 (4%)
> Annual Pay Raise: 3.5%

The Rising Income Strategy

Year	Beginning Savings Value		Investment Earnings		Annual Withdrawal		Reinvestment/ Compounding	Year End Savings Value
1	$500,000	+	$37,500	−	$20,000	=	$17,500	$517,500
2	$517,500	+	$38,813	−	$20,700	=	$18,113	$535,613
3	$535,613	+	$40,171	−	$21,425	=	$18,746	$554,359
4	$554,359	+	$41,577	−	$22,174	=	$19,403	$573,762

Looking at just these first four years of a RI Strategy at work, you can see that Ben Franklin knew what he was talking about. By spending less than you earn and reinvesting the difference, you've put compounding to work *for* you, rather than *against* you, in two ways.

First, your reinvestment is causing your retirement savings to grow over time. Second, your larger retirement savings is generating larger earnings. That's a win-win when it comes to your need for a rising income. Even after giving yourself a 3.5% pay raise to keep up with inflation, compounding continues to work for you.

The Rising Income Strategy heads you in the right direction, giving you an income that keeps up with rising living costs. It's the only one of the three plans we've looked at that is designed to do this. Take a look:

Rising Income Strategy
The only strategy that keeps up

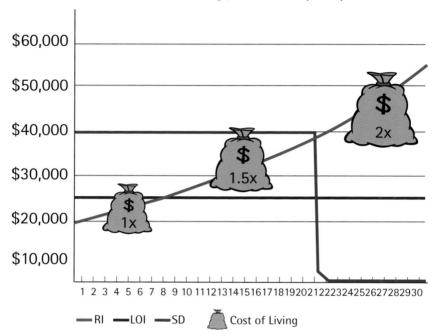

—RI —LOI —SD    Cost of Living

Insights from a Focus Group

When I shared this strategy with participants, I was told, "This looks great, but it's making a big assumption. You're assuming I can earn a steady 7.5% each year and I don't know any investments that can do that right now..."

Do you have the same response? Hold that thought. We'll be dealing with fluctuating investment returns in great detail in Part 3. For now, it's important to understand the function and philosophy of the RI Strategy. We'll begin applying this knowledge to the real world in the next chapter.

The Power of Compounding

We've talked about the power of letting compounding work for you. Want an illustration of just how amazing compounding is during a three-decade retirement when you use the Rising Income Strategy? Check out the magic of this math.

Remember that we said consumer goods in the third decade will cost *twice as much* as they did in the first decade? Well that isn't the end of the story.

Even though living costs in the third decade will have doubled, you'll need only *half* the amount of money that you need in the first decade. Let me say that again: The third decade is going to cost you *half* the money that the first decade cost. *Half!*

How can *that* be?

Let's say you're going to spend $25,000 from your savings each year during your first decade of retirement. That means you'll spend $250,000 over that ten-year period. From this information, you can easily determine your living costs for the third decade. Since everything will cost twice as much, you'll need $500,000.

But didn't I just say that the third decade will require only half the money that the first decade required? Yes, it's true; I'm saying that your third decade will only require $125,000.

When is $125,000 worth $500,000? When it has 20 years to *compound* at 7.5%. (To be more precise, the actual value is $530,981.39). *That* is how the third decade will require only half the money that the first decade did.

Ben Franklin was right — compounding really is the eighth wonder of the world!

The Rising Income Strategy does what its name implies. It's the only strategy designed to give you an income that keeps up with three decades of rising living costs. Managed correctly, a RI Strategy is the only way to never begin running out of money in retirement.

What does never beginning to run out of money look like? The graph below shows the projected value of your retirement savings over time, using each of the three withdrawal strategies. Keep in mind that these are hypothetical examples, based on numbers we've made up. Don't focus on the actual values, but the trends.

Retirement Savings Value Trends

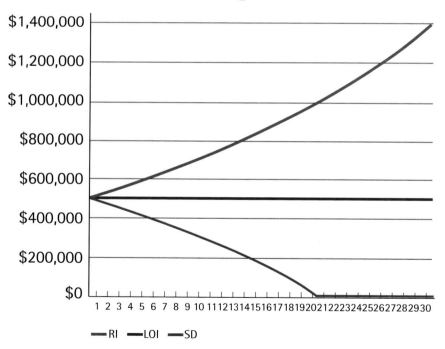

This graph, all by itself, would make you think that both the RI and LOI strategies will keep you from ever running out of money in retirement. But you know better. You know that the LOI Strategy starts eroding your savings in your second and third decades of retirement; at some point you'll be forced to begin spending your principal. When that happens, you'll be following the same cliff-diving downward trend of the SD Strategy shown here.

As I said earlier: If you want to never begin running out of money, you need to grow your nest egg during retirement. Only the RI Strategy does this for you. If your retirement savings is following this upward trend over time, you know you're on the right path.

Origin of the term "Cash Cow"

There's no doubt that a single milk cow can be a real moneymaker.

Think about it. You buy the cow for a relatively low price and then add grass and water. The cow does the rest, producing milk throughout her adult life, meaning a steady "flow" of income for the farmer. It's no wonder a venture that generates profits far exceeding its start-up costs is called a "Cash Cow."

Is It Ever Okay to Start Spending Your Principal?

At this point, you might be thinking, "These numbers look pretty good, but do I really need to grow my savings this much when I'm retired? It seems kind of silly to keep growing my nest egg when I might only have a few years left."

What you're really asking is "When is it okay to go off the cliff?" The best I can say is that it's okay to go off the cliff and begin spending your principal whenever you're ready to start losing the things that make retirement great.

But if you still think that growing your retirement savings when you might only have a few years left is overkill, let me ask you this: What if we both have a blind spot and it turns out that you'll be hanging in there for a fourth decade of retirement?

That is why you must keep growing your savings.

Insights from a Focus Group

A question I was asked by my participants is, "Chuck, according to your graph, with the Rising Income Strategy I've got a $1 million nest egg in my third decade of retirement. Why do I need that much money when I'm that old? Can't I begin spending some of my principal at that point?"

Do you wonder that yourself? The answer is that you won't feel as wealthy as you think. At 3.5% inflation, that $1 million in your third decade of retirement will have the same purchasing power as $500,000 did at the beginning of your retirement. All you've done by growing your nest egg is keep up with inflation.

Face it. If you do this right, you're going to die with money left. That's the point. Is this starting to seem like a good idea to you?

The Lifestyle Path

"When you have confidence, you can have a lot of fun.
And when you have fun, you can do amazing things."

- Joe Namath

The path of the RI Strategy is one of financial confidence — confidence in the future that provides confidence in the present.

Given that your retirement savings will be keeping pace with the rising cost of living, you'll always feel as wealthy as you did on the first day of your retirement. You'll be able to spend time and money on pursuits that are meaningful to you. For you, this might mean enjoying quality time with family or supporting worthwhile community causes. Or maybe you want to explore a long delayed passion for travel, music, writing, or a brand new hobby. Instead of cramping your style, your financial situation will support these activities. When you're on top of your retirement mountain with no fear of going over the cliff, you can enjoy all the good stuff that retirement offers.

Let's talk about the later years…the ones you worry about most. What if your health fails you? What if you can't care for yourself? While the RI Strategy can't change this outcome, it can make these years much more comfortable. By arriving at the third decade with the same amount of purchasing power you had in the first decade, you'll be able to afford quality care — more so than you would with any other strategy. This strategy gives you flexibility. Choices. More importantly, it gives your loved ones the ability to care for you without creating a financial hardship for them at an already difficult time.

What happens when you reach the end of your path? Well, if you've done it right, you're going to die with money left over. You're going to have the opportunity to make a meaningful difference to people or causes that you care about. I've talked with enough retired clients to know that it feels good to give back, at any age.

Happy Cows Make More Milk

A recent English university study advised dairy farmers to name their cows. The researchers claim that simply calling a cow by name makes Buttercup and Felicity and MooMoo feel special. So why is this important? Because happy, relaxed cows produce more milk — in fact, almost 500 pints more milk each year!

The RI Strategy meets all three criteria. Enough said.

Money Doesn't Buy You Happiness...Or Does It?

Getting older means getting happier. Recent research has shown that people all over the world, regardless of culture or location, tend to get happier as they age. After reaching a low at the age of 46, a person's level of happiness rises for the rest of their life.[1] This means that retirees have a 20-year head start in the happiness department.

Why is this meaningful? Because doctors long ago observed a link between happiness and health. Happier people tend to be healthier people. So if you want to live a long time, be happy. Said another way, make it a personal mission to avoid unhappiness.

I suggest a good place to start is to dispel the old myth that "money doesn't buy you happiness." Research has shown that this is simply untrue. Not surprisingly, there is a direct link between our level of income and our level of happiness and satisfaction in life.[2] It's only logical that this relationship exists when you consider the alternative...imagine a life with a lack of money. How happy does that sound?

Despite the results you have seen, the goal of the Rising Income Strategy isn't to make you rich...it is to prevent financial hardship in your retirement. It is to allow you to maintain your standard of living, no matter how long you live. It is to enable you to maintain your trend toward greater happiness throughout your golden years.

Insights from a Focus Group

"Not everyone can afford this strategy...only paying themselves 4% of their retirement savings to start out."

I heard this comment more than once as I met with focus groups to discuss these retirement withdrawal strategies. What can I say but, "You're right, many people can't"?

I am fully aware of this fact. We all know people who have suffered downturns in their lives that have affected them financially. Maybe they suffered a job loss, or had unexpected medical bills. Or maybe they just spent too much and didn't save enough for retirement. Whatever the case, the facts about retirement income don't change.

I can't change the markets or inflation or ever-improving healthcare. I can't keep people who can't afford to begin retirement with a 4% withdrawal, or choose not to, safely on the mountain. The truth is, as you'll see in a coming example, withdrawing more than 4% when you begin a three-decade retirement means forgoing the luxury of having the confidence that you will never begin to run out of money.

On the flip side, there are plenty of people who CAN afford to start out retirement with a 4% withdrawal rate. These are people that have made prudent financial choices so that they can enjoy their retirement with the lifestyle they desire, or people who have had good fortune smile upon them. Regardless, they still have blind spots. They will need the information in this book to maintain the solid financial foundation they worked so long to build.

I wish I could help everyone, but I've been working as a retirement planner long enough to know that I cannot. I can only help those who have a desire to help themselves. When their blind spots are revealed and they understand the facts, many people will discover that they need to work longer than they thought to afford a retirement in which they never begin to run out of money.

Is it worth it? Imagine a retirement with, and then without financial worries to find your answer.

Summary

The Rising Income Strategy works. It makes compounding work for you as powerfully as inflation makes compounding work against you. The strategy is simple: Spend less than you earn and reinvest the rest. It's the only way to make your savings grow during your retirement. And growing your savings isn't optional if you want to never begin running out of money.

The path you'll find yourself on is the one most retirees dream about — confidently living each year, knowing that you're in control of your financial future. You'll experience a sense of freedom and independence. It's the path that leads you to the greatest views that the retirement mountain has to offer.

Next up: If the RI Strategy is clearly the best choice for your retirement years, why don't more retirees choose it? Because they don't believe it really works. Retirees realize that no investment can promise the same high returns each year for three decades. They know that investments fluctuate. And it's this fluctuation that makes them choose something they think is "safer," like the LOI Strategy. Because many retirees aren't comfortable with the investments that the Rising Income Strategy requires you to make, we need to talk about how to apply this strategy in a world of fluctuating investment returns. In Part 3, we'll figure out exactly how to make the RI strategy work for you.

Manage Your Withdrawal Strategy Appropriately

Part 3

Now that you've learned what your blind spots are and know how to choose the right retirement strategy that adjusts for these blind spots, it's time to learn how to manage your withdrawal strategy appropriately. Part 3 introduces a powerful tool to help you determine how much you can withdraw from your retirement savings at the beginning of your retirement, as well as each year after that. You'll also learn a simple strategy for managing your withdrawal strategy appropriately throughout changing economic conditions so you can be confident that you'll never begin running out of money.

Then, sit in on two client sessions to see firsthand what considerations are involved in setting up a retirement withdrawal strategy and in adjusting a withdrawal strategy that is heading for trouble as you explore the benefits of working with a financial planner.

Turn the page to learn more. Chapter 8 will tell you what you need to know to stay on your mountain despite fluctuating investment returns. Chapter 9 will give you a magic number to use to help protect your nest egg against unlucky fluctuation. Chapter 10 will allow you to assess whether you are in danger of running out of money in your retirement. Chapter 11 will show you how you can work to eliminate the risk of taking a pay cut during retirement. Chapter 12 provides two real life examples of retirement in action, and, lastly, in Chapter 13, we'll discuss facing the future with faith, not fear.

Manage Your Withdrawal Strategy Appropriately

Rising Income in the Real World

Let's quickly review the three steps for living a financially successful retirement, one in which you'll never begin running out of money:

1. Know your blind spots.
2. Choose a withdrawal strategy that adjusts for these blind spots.
3. Manage your withdrawal strategy appropriately.

As you've just seen, the Rising Income Strategy is the only strategy that adjusts for your blind spots. Of the three withdrawal strategies we've looked at, the RI Strategy is the only one that gives you an income that grows over time so that you never begin to run out of money.

But maybe you thought that the Rising Income Strategy example seemed a little "too perfect." Nothing works out that predictably in the real world.

You're right. It doesn't. So now that you've got the basics of withdrawal strategies down pat, it's time to step up our discussion a notch and proceed to Step 3: Manage your withdrawal strategy appropriately. The real world isn't at all like our steady and predictable example in Chapter 7.

> " To **manage** your RI Strategy you need a **plan** for dealing with **fluctuation**. "

99

Getting Up To Speed On Financial Terms And Investment Options

Returns/Earnings: The amount of income or growth that your portfolio generates over a specified time period. The examples in this book use an annual return. The portfolio in the Rising Income example earned 7.5% each year. Said another way, the portfolio had a 7.5% return each year.

Withdrawal: The periodic amount of income you take from your nest egg. Some people choose to take a steady amount of money from their nest egg each month, while others take a lump sum withdrawal each year. The timing of your withdrawal depends on your needs. For the examples in this book, withdrawals are taken at the end of each year, giving the portfolio a chance to generate earnings throughout the year.

Fixed Income (FI) Portfolio: A portfolio comprised of investments that pay a fixed rate of interest. They are designed to earn a predictable, non-changing amount of interest each year. Typical investments in this category include Bank Certificates of Deposit (CD's) and bonds.

Growth and Income (G&I) Portfolio: A portfolio comprised of both growth investments (stocks) and fixed income investments (bonds/CD's). A typical G&I Portfolio is comprised of at least 60% growth investments with the remainder in fixed income investments. A G&I portfolio does not provide a guaranteed rate of growth.

Stocks: Portions of ownership in a corporation. The value of your investment goes up and down, depending on the price of the stock, which is influenced by the earnings that the corporation generates.

Bonds: Loans to a corporation or government entity. Bonds are typically structured to pay the bondholder a specific rate of interest for a specific period of time. Bonds are included in the fixed income investment category.

Fluctuation: Changes, both up and down, in the value of your investments. For example, investments in a G&I portfolio will generate returns that will be different each and every year.

A discussion of specific investment allocations and portfolio management for retirees is beyond the scope of this book. With the investment options for retirees growing each year, I recommend working with a professional financial advisor to design a portfolio customized to meet your income needs.

The F-word

The Rising Income Strategy calls for a different kind of investment than the other two strategies require. Your savings need to be invested in a growth and income (G&I) portfolio, rather than in a fixed income (FI) portfolio. The G&I portfolio gives you the potential for higher returns over time. These higher returns are necessary to get compounding to work for you as powerfully as inflation is making it work against you. But with these higher returns comes something else. It's the dreaded F-word...*fluctuation*.

Maybe you were skeptical about our example in the previous chapter. It showed retirement savings earning a steady 7.5% return each year. From real world experience, you may know that G&I portfolios don't give predictably high returns year after year. That's because G&I portfolios include both stocks and bonds. And stock markets fluctuate. They don't go up at a steady rate year after year. They go up a little...and down a little...and sometimes they go up and down a lot.

Our Rising Income Strategy example might be scientifically accurate, based on the average long-term returns of G&I portfolios, but it's not what you're likely to experience in the real world. To manage your RI Strategy, you'll need a plan for dealing with fluctuation.

For most retirees, "fluctuation" is a very scary word. They equate fluctuation with *loss*. This one-sided thinking leads to another F-word...*fear*. And fear is a dangerous emotion when it comes to investing. It causes over-cautious investors to make decisions that help them feel good in the short run, even though those decisions may cause them financial hardship in the long run.

Fear of fluctuation is a common reason that retirees choose a Living Off the Interest Strategy, putting all their savings in investments that yield a fixed income, **even** though this strategy is designed to fail in a 21ˢᵗ century retirement. Retirees are comforted by the idea that FI investments are guaranteed not to fluctuate. The problem, of course, is that they are also guaranteed not to grow.

Remember what our retirees said:

"I want to protect my principal and live off the interest."

"I don't want any investments that can lose money."

"If I can earn 5% interest, that'll be fine. Give me something stable."

"I want an income that's guaranteed not to change."

"Just keep the value of my savings the same; that way I'll be able to sleep at night."

These are all ways of saying, "I'm afraid of fluctuation, because it means that I'll lose my money and become poor in retirement."

And so the rationalization begins. It goes something like this:

"I like the LOI Strategy because I know it won't fluctuate at all, so I don't have to worry about losing my money. Sure, I guess it's possible that I'll become poorer as time goes on, but I don't expect to live that long (BLIND SPOT!), so the LOI Strategy seems like a safer plan for me."

OR

"I like that my investments won't fluctuate, and in the second decade I'm planning on not spending much anyway. (BLIND SPOT!) I really won't need to travel and I'll probably be able to reduce my expenses."

OR

"By the time I reach the second decade, I'll feel more comfortable spending some of my principal if I need to because I just won't have that many more years left." (BLIND SPOT!)

OR

"I would rather have the peace of mind today. I'll just figure it out later. Nobody knows what the future has in store for us." Okay, that's not a blind spot, it's flat out DENIAL. Like death and taxes, inflation is pretty darn sure to keep coming, no matter how much we'd rather avoid it.

Fear of fluctuation is a powerful force. It's what causes financially smart retirees to choose a path that may lead them straight off the retirement mountain cliff. For most people, today's fluctuation is much scarier than tomorrow's rising living costs. *The fear of loss overrides the hope for gain.*

But is this fear of fluctuation rational? Remember that fluctuation isn't about loss; it's about, well…fluctuation.

What Is Fluctuation, Really?

Let's step back and take a good, hard look at what fluctuation is. In everyday terms, it refers to a movement that goes up and down. If I'm counting correctly, that's *two* directions. When applied to the stock market, values fluctuate in both directions…up and down. So there's upside fluctuation and there's downside fluctuation.

Most people — retirees in particular — get so fixated on the *down* that they forget the *up*. They don't stop to consider that fluctuation is a good and necessary thing for pulling off higher investment returns.

Fluctuation is the reason the high returns exist in the first place. You're paid greater returns from G&I portfolios (over guaranteed fixed rate investments) as a reward for agreeing to put up with the short-term fluctuations of the stock market. Fluctuation isn't a bad thing, it's a necessary thing. And in the end, it's a good thing because it's going to give you the investment returns you need to keep up with three decades of rising living costs.

Try this on: Fluctuation is a *good* thing.

90 Years of Fluctuation

To illustrate the idea of fluctuation being a good thing, let's take a quick look at the Dow Jones Industrial Average since 1920.

Dow Jones Industrial Average (1920–2010)

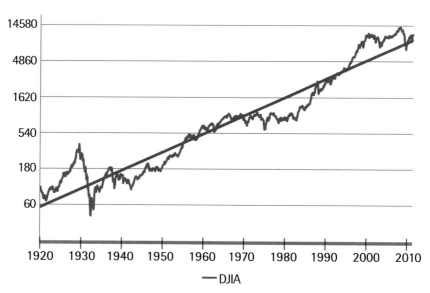

— DJIA

Source: Dow Jones[1]
Data shown in log scale to best illustrate long term index patterns. Past performance is no guarantee of future results. Chart is for illustrative purposes only.

Even with all the short-term fluctuation, you can see a simple, even predictable pattern…up. Over the *long-term,* it's clear that fluctuation really isn't a problem at all. But let's be honest, the long-term isn't your main concern, is it? Nobody ever worries about the permanent upward trend of the market. I've yet to get a call from a client who was concerned that his portfolio had gone up 20% in a particular year. The calls only come in when the market goes down.

It's the *short-term* downside fluctuation that concerns you. You don't care what happened over the last 90 years. All you care about is what will happen over the next 30 years. Heck, if you are like most retirees, you are more worried about the next year than you are the next decade.

This fear of short-term fluctuation is understandable; it creates a real world planning challenge.

The Planning Challenge

Our rising income example in Chapter 7 used a steady year-after-year average return of 7.5% for its annual growth calculations. This doesn't reflect what really happens — you can expect short-term fluctuations during your three-decade retirement. Your real returns each year will differ quite a bit from the average.

With a Rising Income Strategy, in which your retirement savings are invested in a G&I Portfolio, you can expect your annual return to be either higher or lower than 7.5%. But over time, if history keeps repeating itself, it's reasonable to assume your return will average out to about 7.5% per year.

The following Table of Fluctuating Returns is a collection of 30 hypothetical annual returns. The table is meant to illustrate the random possibility of returns, not the promise of any specific return. These returns are not from a specific time period or investment. They are used here to illustrate the mathematical impact that fluctuating investment returns might have on your nest egg when you begin taking regularly scheduled withdrawals.

This collection of returns includes both *bear markets* (markets that went down) and *bull markets* (markets that went up). And did you notice? There's not a 7.5% return anywhere on the board. Still, you can put all 30 of these returns together in any order and you'll always end up with an average return of 7.5%.

Table of Fluctuating Returns		
17.60%	13.21%	-30.00%
24.12%	-8.92%	31.59%
27.71%	27.70%	16.76%
-3.35%	7.87%	18.17%
32.77%	13.21%	-7.46%
17.02%	-3.80%	18.18%
13.51%	7.89%	14.32%
9.15%	0.12%	31.14%
-24.65%	37.08%	-25.13%
-4.86%	18.19%	-16.22%

Average: 7.5%

The Sequence of Returns Doesn't Matter...when you are saving a lump sum:

If you had invested $10,000 for retirement 30 years ago in a G&I portfolio that produced an average 7.5% return for you over that time period, you would have almost $88,000 today. To illustrate that the sequence of returns doesn't matter in this scenario, I've put the returns from our Table of Fluctuating Returns in forward and reverse order. Even though each experience is slightly different, the end result is the same. Both scenarios accumulated $87,794, because they both had the same 7.5% average return.

Turning $10,000 into $87,974 over 30 years means you earned an average return of 7.5%.

		Forward			Reverse
		$10,000			$10,000
1	17.60%	$11,760	30	-16.22%	$8,378
2	24.12%	$14,596	29	-25.13%	$6,273
3	27.71%	$18,640	28	31.14%	$8,226
4	-3.35%	$18,016	27	14.32%	$9,404
5	32.77%	$23,920	26	18.18%	$11,113
6	17.02%	$27,992	25	-7.46%	$10,284
7	13.51%	$31,774	24	18.17%	$12,153
8	9.15%	$34,680	23	16.76%	$14,190
9	-24.65%	$26,132	22	31.59%	$18,673
10	-4.86%	$24,861	21	-30.00%	$13,072
11	13.21%	$28,145	20	18.19%	$15,449
12	-8.92%	$25,636	19	37.08%	$21,178
13	27.70%	$32,736	18	0.12%	$21,204
14	7.87%	$35,313	17	7.89%	$22,876
15	13.21%	$39,976	16	-3.80%	$22,007
16	-3.80%	$38,457	15	13.21%	$24,913
17	7.89%	$41,490	14	7.87%	$26,874
18	0.12%	$41,541	13	27.70%	$34,317
19	37.08%	$56,945	12	-8.92%	$31,258
20	18.19%	$67,301	11	13.21%	$35,386
21	-30.00%	$47,114	10	-4.86%	$33,665
22	31.59%	$61,998	9	-24.65%	$25,368
23	16.76%	$72,388	8	9.15%	$27,687
24	18.17%	$85,543	7	13.51%	$31,429
25	-7.46%	$79,161	6	17.02%	$36,778
26	18.18%	$93,553	5	32.77%	$48,831
27	14.32%	$106,947	4	-3.35%	$47,197
28	31.14%	$140,248	3	27.71%	$60,275
29	-25.13%	$105,005	2	24.12%	$74,810
30	-16.22%	**$87,974**	1	17.60%	**$87,974**

In the real world, since every G&I portfolio will likely experience returns both higher and lower than 7.5% from year to year, using an average return can create an unrealistic picture of just how the Rising Income Strategy will work for you.

What will your real world returns be? And in what order will they come?

These questions highlight the planning challenge created by fluctuation. But it's a challenge that can be overcome. The first step is to understand the impact that short-term downside fluctuation can have on your RI Strategy. Because it matters...sometimes.

Origin of Bull Market (Bear Market)

The historic origin of the terms "bull market" and "bear market" is unclear, but there are several present-day explanations that pair these animals with the financial conditions they represent. For example, when they attack, a bull forces his horns upward while a bear swipes his paws downward. In terms of their speed, bulls charge with great force while bears lumber. Participants in a bull market are often referred to as a "herd."

A Short History Of Short-Term Fluctuation:

Question: What causes short-term downside fluctuation in growth portfolios?

Answer: Bear markets

The good news about bear markets is that they are usually much shorter than bull markets. Since World War II, the stock market has experienced a bear market about once every 4-5 years. These bear markets lasted, on average, about 15 months. The bull markets, on the other hand, lasted about five years.

Tying these statistics to your own three-decade retirement, it's reasonable for you to expect to experience about six bear markets during your golden years. If history repeats itself, that means you might see about four or five positive annual returns for every one negative annual return.

We won't know when the bear markets will happen or how long they'll last. And we can't predict how much downside fluctuation you'll experience before the markets resume their long-term upward climb.

But we don't really need to know...if we manage your RI Strategy well.

Source: Dow Jones

This isn't Las Vegas, it's your retirement.

How can fluctuation matter only sometimes? Well, in a matter of speaking, it comes down to how lucky you are when you retire.

Let's look at two retirees who have exactly the same Rising Income Strategy, but different "luck" when they retire at the youthful age of 60. In our example, both retirees start with $500,000 invested in a G&I portfolio. They both begin by taking a $20,000 withdrawal in their first year of retirement. Each year, they give themselves a 3.5% pay raise to keep up with inflation. And they both have the same average return (7.5%) over their 30-year retirement.

You're probably thinking that this sounds exactly like the rising income example from Chapter 7. You're right. Except now, we're going to apply real world returns. Now, instead of analyzing a theoretical G&I portfolio earning a steady 7.5% return year after year, we're going to apply *fluctuating* returns — just like those encountered in the real world. In fact, let's use the returns from our *Table of Fluctuating Returns* and see how the numbers play out.

Holy Cow Casino and Brewery — first microbrewery in Las Vegas.

Established in 1993, The Holy Cow Casino and Brewery was the first microbrewery in Las Vegas. Imagine sitting at the cow-themed bar, downing a brewski poured from the nine-tap milk can tower. The place was open 24 hours, so you could stay until the cows came home. House beers included Holy Cow Dunkelweizen, Holy Cow Sweet Stout, and Holy Cow Amber Gambler Pale Ale. They just don't brew 'em like that anymore — Las Vegas' original brewpub closed in 2002.

Meet Ms. Lucky

Our first investor, Ms. Lucky, will experience the investment returns in exactly the same order listed on the chalkboard in our Table of Fluctuating Returns.

And here are the results of the first three decades of Ms. Lucky's RI Strategy:

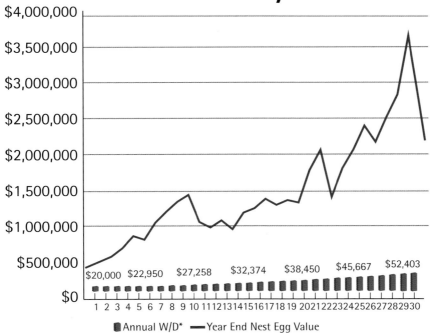

Ms. Lucky

$20,000 $22,950 $27,258 $32,374 $38,450 $45,667 $52,403

■ Annual W/D* ━ Year End Nest Egg Value

*Annual Withdrawal not to scale

Success! Even with fluctuation, over time Ms. Lucky was able to pay herself a rising income to keep up with inflation. Better yet, she was able to grow her nest egg. In fact, in her 30th year, she's paying herself more than double the income she started with in her first year of retirement. Her original nest egg, even after a bear market in the last two years, has quadrupled.

Ms. Lucky achieved her goal of a financially successful retirement in which she never begins to run out of money. You go, Ms. Lucky! This stuff really works.

But not so fast…

Meet Mr. Unlucky

Let's now take a look at Mr. Unlucky. He has exactly the same Rising Income Strategy as the one Ms. Lucky used to ace her three decades of retirement. (And by the way, she's now in her fourth decade.) But in his case, we're going to make a small change…not to his plan, but to his fluctuation.

Let's use the same set of returns from our Table of Fluctuating Returns that we used with Ms. Lucky, but let's put them in reverse order. The return Mr. Unlucky will experience in Year 1 (-16.22%) is the same return that Ms. Lucky experienced in Year 30. Remember, reversing the order doesn't change the average return over the 30 years; so even with this change, he will have the same average return of 7.5%.

Since he's using the same strategy and earning the same 7.5% average return, he should be as successful as Ms. Lucky, right? Well, let's just say he's not named Mr. Unlucky for nothing. Changing the order of the returns changes everything:

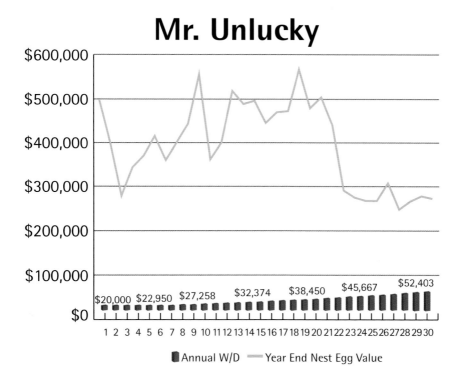

Mr. Unlucky

Annual W/D ▬ Year End Nest Egg Value

Holy cow, what a difference. This doesn't look good at all. It's true that Mr. Unlucky is able to pay himself a rising income and that he doesn't run out of money, but look at what's happening to the value of his nest egg during the last decade. It's running out! It is worth about half of its original value. Not a good situation in a world where the cost of living has doubled. If our objective is to never begin running out of money (and by now, you know that it is), then this plan is a real loser.

What's Going On Here?

In our example, both retirees had an average return of 7.5% over 30 years. Both also saw the same number and magnitude of bull markets and bear markets. The only difference was the timing.

The lesson here?

The timing of fluctuation matters. Or to be specific, the timing of *downside fluctuation* matters.

The key difference in our examples is that Mr. Unlucky experienced a bear market during the first two years of his retirement and Ms. Lucky didn't. This early bear market hurt his plan more because it affected his strategy for a longer period of time. Just like inflation gets worse the longer it's around (compounding), downside fluctuation hurts more when it happens early. Its impact has more years to echo throughout your retirement.

Ms. Lucky experienced these same bear markets much later in her retirement. But in her case, they didn't create a problem. That's because her G&I portfolio had time to build up a cushion before it ran into its first setback. This softened the double impact of the bear market and Ms. Lucky's withdrawals. On the other hand, Mr. Unlucky's early bear market, combined with his withdrawals, was just too much. The bull markets of the later years weren't enough to overcome these previous setbacks.

Bear markets affect you differently depending on how early or late you run into them during your retirement. Unfortunately, you don't have any way of knowing when you'll experience these temporary downside fluctuations in retirement.

So to sum it up, making the RI Strategy work comes down to luck...right?

Wrong. Because there *is* a way to help shield your long-term strategy against short-term downside fluctuation. The real lesson here is that you need to protect yourself against unlucky timing... especially in the early years. Remember, fluctuation isn't bad; in fact, it's necessary. It just needs to be managed.

Summary

Fluctuation is a fact of life when it comes to investments. There's upside fluctuation and there's downside fluctuation; there are bull markets and there are bear markets. It's all part of the real world financial cycle.

To stand any chance of keeping up in a three-decade retirement, you need, not a Fixed Income Portfolio, but a Growth and Income Portfolio. And the real world of fluctuating markets can present a planning challenge for the Rising Income Strategy.

Sometimes, that is.

Early bear markets (unlucky fluctuation) put more stress on your RI strategy than it may be able to handle over a 30-year retirement. It's not all that comforting to know that the Rising Income strategy works only when you have lucky timing, at least when it comes to bear and bull markets.

Next Up: Who knows if you'll be one of the lucky ones? Relying on luck is no way to plan for a financially successful retirement. For security, once you've retired, there must be a way to manage your plan that protects you against the possibility of unlucky fluctuation. Luck just shouldn't be a factor in your strategy for never beginning to run out of money in retirement.

Fret not, help is on the way. You *can't* control the fluctuation that you experience, but you *can* manage it. You're about to learn a simple, but powerful tool for protecting your Rising Income Strategy against unlucky fluctuation. Learning to use this tool will give you confidence that you'll be able to stay comfortably on your retirement mountain. It will keep you safely on your path, never venturing close to the cliff's edge.

Starting Off on the Right Path

Taking Luck Out of It

Nobody wants to keep their fingers crossed for three decades of retirement, hoping they happen to be among the "lucky" ones who dodge an early bear market. Heck, that LOI Strategy is starting to look kind of appealing again, isn't it? STOP IT!! That thing is leading you off the cliff. The Rising Income Strategy doesn't...provided you know how to *manage* it.

And you're now ready to learn about a powerful tool that will help you do just that. You can think of this tool as the "magic number" that holds the key to your financial planning success. Manage this number well, and you'll never begin running out of money during retirement. With this magic number, you are about to take luck right out of the equation, so that *you* can control your destiny with the RI Strategy over a three-decade (or more) retirement. This number can put you on a safe path, far away from the cliff's edge. Okay, so what is this magic number?

> " How **much** you pay yourself in the **first** year of retirement makes all the difference. "

It's your *withdrawal rate* (W/D rate).

W/D rates are your key to success when using the RI Strategy. They help you in two ways. First, they get you started on the right foot in retirement by telling you how much you can afford to pay yourself from your nest egg. Second, they're an ever-present guide for helping you gauge the luckiness or unluckiness of the fluctuation your RI Strategy is experiencing. W/D rates keep you safely on your path, never venturing close to the cliff's edge.

Let's begin by defining what this magic number of a W/D rate is and then talk about just how you're going to use this powerful tool.

The Simple Math of Withdrawal Rates

Your W/D rate represents the pace at which you're taking an income from your nest egg. It's easy to calculate — you only need two numbers:

> **1. Your Annual Withdrawal Amount (AWA)** – how much (as in, *a specific dollar amount*) do you plan to take out of your nest egg this year?
>
> **2. Your Nest Egg Value (NEV)** – how much money do you have in your retirement savings right now?
>
> Simply divide the first number by the second number and you have your W/D rate.

You may recall that, in Chapter 7, I suggested that you take a 4% withdrawal your first year if you retire at age 62. That 4% is your initial W/D rate, as you can see on the chalkboard.

This is also the example from the first year of Ms. Lucky's and Mr. Unlucky's Rising Income Strategy. If you remember, they both planned to take a $20,000 withdrawal in the first year of retirement and they both started off with a nest egg value of $500,000. By using our simple formula, it's easy to determine that they both started off retirement with a W/D rate of 4%.

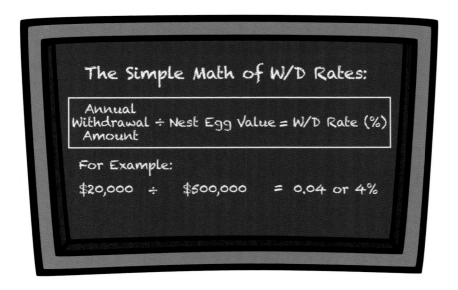

The Simple Math of W/D Rates:

$$\text{Annual Withdrawal Amount} \div \text{Nest Egg Value} = \text{W/D Rate (\%)}$$

For Example:

$$\$20,000 \div \$500,000 = 0.04 \text{ or } 4\%$$

What's interesting (and instructive) about the Ms. Lucky/ Mr. Unlucky example is that this *first* year of their retirements was also the *last* year that their withdrawal rates would ever be the same. That's because the W/D rate is a math formula with an important variable — the nest egg value. That variable (remember how, due to fluctuation, it can go down as well as up?) becomes especially important when it's *your* nest egg value.

W/D Rates in Motion

The funny thing about W/D rates is that, when you're using a RI Strategy, they don't stay constant. Why? There are actually, not one, but two variables involved. Because each year, both your *annual withdrawal amount* and your *nest egg value* are changing.

Think about it…you plan to take just a little bit more income each year to keep up with inflation, so your *annual withdrawal amount* is always going up. Also, your *nest egg value* is going to fluctuate, based on the returns you earn with your G&I portfolio. In any given year, your nest egg could be worth more or less than the year before. (Before you start to panic again, remember that historically, you'll have more *up* years than *down* years).

With both your AWAs and NEVs changing each and every year, your W/D rate will be changing every year too.

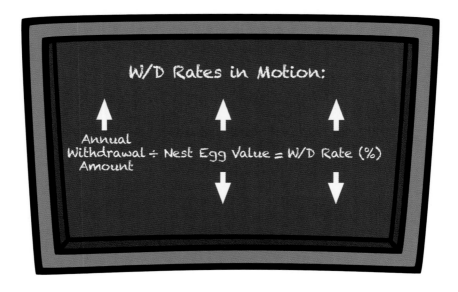

To see how these ever-changing values result in a changing withdrawal rate, let's revisit Ms. Lucky and Mr. Unlucky and check out their withdrawal rates at the mid-points of their three-decade retirements.

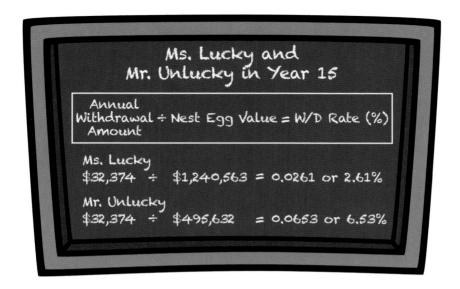

Ms. Lucky and Mr. Unlucky in Year 15

| Annual Withdrawal Amount | ÷ | Nest Egg Value | = | W/D Rate (%) |

Ms. Lucky
$32,374 ÷ $1,240,563 = 0.0261 or 2.61%

Mr. Unlucky
$32,374 ÷ $495,632 = 0.0653 or 6.53%

Starting with Ms. Lucky, we discover something interesting. After 15 years of increasing income and market fluctuation, her W/D rate has, interestingly, gone down. She's taking about 1.6x more income in Year 15 than she did in her first year of her retirement, but her W/D rate is now only 2.61%. That's because the value of her nest egg has grown over those 15 years. If she hadn't grown her nest egg as much (or at all), her W/D rate would have been higher. Like Mr. Unlucky's, for instance.

In Mr. Unlucky's 15th year of retirement, he's taking the same income as Ms. Lucky, but at 6.53%, his W/D rate is higher than hers. That's because his nest egg didn't grow like hers did, because of that unlucky bear market early in his retirement.

So the same Rising Income Strategy gave us two different W/D rates — all because of market fluctuation.

Now that you understand what W/D rates are and how to calculate them, let's discuss how you can use them.

A GPS for Your Rising Income Strategy

Withdrawal rates don't just start you off in the right direction; they tell you how to stay on the right path...and away from the cliff's edge. Think of them as a GPS for your RI Strategy. Your W/D rates tell you what's currently happening with your RI Strategy and where you're headed in the future. They serve as an ever-present guide throughout your retirement.

Withdrawal rates help you answer the two most important financial questions every retiree has:

1. How much can I afford to pay myself when I retire?
2. Am I in danger of running out of money in my retirement?

Those are big questions. By learning how to use W/D rates, you'll know how to manage your Rising Income Strategy and protect against unlucky fluctuation.

So, keep reading. This is the good stuff.

Starting Off on the Right Path

You take the first step in protecting against unlucky fluctuation on the day you retire. How much you pay yourself in that very first year of retirement makes all the difference; it determines where you'll be later in your retirement. Will you still be content and confident, enjoying the good life on your retirement mountain? Or will you be living on the edge of the cliff — watching every step, hoping that you won't begin running out of money?

To start your retirement on a safe path, it's important that you answer this question correctly:

How much can I afford to pay myself when I retire?

As we've said, W/D rates hold the answer. In fact, whenever a client asks me this question, my financial planner ears actually hear this:

What is a safe beginning W/D rate for me?

The financial planning industry has conducted a huge amount of research on beginning withdrawal rates. It has studied every retirement income strategy you can imagine, using every withdrawal rate you can imagine, and every type of market fluctuation you can imagine — just to see how it all plays out. Insurance company actuaries, mathematics PhDs, and nerdy financial advisors like me all agree: Your beginning W/D rate depends on your *age*.

The table below tells you, based on your age, how much you can afford to take out of your nest egg at the beginning of your retirement to reduce the possibility of unlucky fluctuation causing you to run out of money.

Starting off on the Right Path

Age	Recommended Beginning W/D rate
55-59	3.5%
60-69	4%
70-79	5%
80+	6.5%

The older you are when you retire, the more you can afford to withdraw. This makes perfect sense when you think about it. You won't need to take an income from your retirement savings portfolio for as many years as a younger retiree would. Put another way, you have fewer years left before you die. That's a morbid way to look at it, I know, but numbers don't lie. They may be insensitive, but they don't lie.

Your age is directly tied to the probability of your running out of money in retirement. The fewer years you have in front of you, the less likely it is that unlucky fluctuation will cause you to run out of money. That's why we base W/D rates on your age.

The more *time* unlucky fluctuation has to impact your strategy, the more *power* it has to take you off your path. Remember the early bear market that Mr. Unlucky experienced? Ms. Lucky experienced that very same bear market, but at the *end* of her retirement — not at the *beginning*. The fact that Mr. U had that unlucky fluctuation during the first two years of his retirement meant that it had a full *three decades* to compound its impact on his RI Strategy.

The probability of unlucky fluctuation causing you to run out of money gets smaller as you age — you have fewer years left to fund. If you only need to pay yourself for 10 years, then fluctuation really isn't much of a factor. It starts becoming a factor when you need to pay for 20 or 30 years of retirement.

To make unlucky fluctuation less of a factor, you need a lower W/D rate — the more years you'll be retired, the lower your beginning W/D rate should be. You need to give yourself a cushion…a bit of insurance. The lower your beginning W/D rate, the more insurance you're giving yourself against unlucky fluctuation.

Using the right W/D rate as you begin your retirement is your first step in protecting yourself against unlucky fluctuation.

Step Number One For Protecting Against Unlucky Fluctuation:
Start Retirement With The Right W/D Rate

You can lead a cow up a stairwell, but not down a stairwell.
Cows can walk up steps, but their knees can't bend properly to walk back down. This fact is fodder for a classic senior prank in rural America: leading a cow upstairs to the high school's second level and leaving her there overnight. Moo-ving the 1,000-pound animal out of the building in the morning usually causes school officials to have a cow and puts participating students in deep manure with authorities. And the cow isn't very happy either.

Don't Cheat the Research

The most dangerous thing you can do as a new retiree is begin with a W/D rate that's too high. It will take too much income from your nest egg. Your nest egg needs to grow at a rate that gives you an income *and* leaves enough money to reinvest, allowing you to keep up with compounding inflation.

Let's be honest — investing is an imperfect science. And an early bear market can change the game.

It's fairly easy to make your money last for a decade. A caveman could do it…or even a cow. It's much harder to make your money last for two or three decades. The recommended beginning W/D rates are designed to reduce the likelihood of a portfolio running out of money because of unlucky fluctuation.

Let's look at Ms. Lucky and Mr. Unlucky again. Both of them started their retirements with a beginning W/D rate of 4%. Neither of them ran out of money during their three decades. But what would have happened if they started with a beginning W/D rate of 5% (higher than what is recommended)?

Nest Egg Values using a 5% Beginning W/D Rate

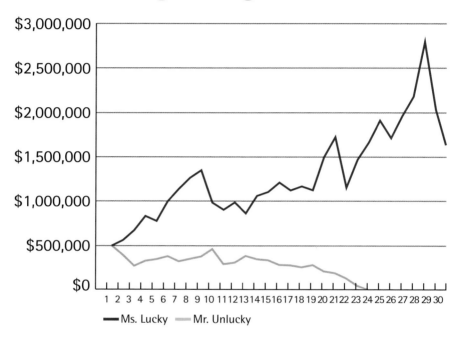

Ms. Lucky ▬▬ Mr. Unlucky

That orange line you see going to *zero* in year 24...that's poor Mr. Unlucky running out of money during his retirement. You can almost see him plunging off the steep orange-lined cliff. All because he started off with a 5% W/D rate instead of a 4% rate. And that's why your beginning W/D rate is so important.

Remember what we're trying to protect against here...unlucky fluctuation. If you have lucky fluctuation, your beginning W/D rate isn't nearly as much of a factor. Just take a look at Ms. Lucky: Even with a 5% beginning W/D rate, she has a $1.6 million nest egg in her 30th year of retirement.

Now you understand why I used a 4% W/D rate when I introduced you to the Rising Income Strategy. That particular rate made a difference. Just look at how it affected Mr. Unlucky:

Mr. Unlucky's Nest Egg Values

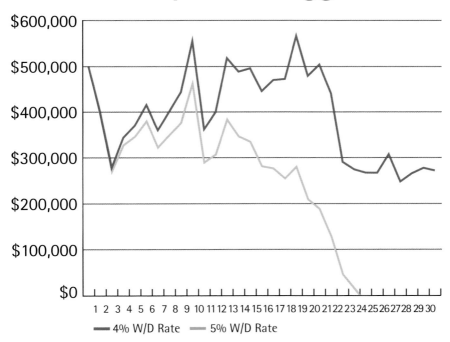

By starting off his retirement with a beginning W/D rate of 4%, Mr. Unlucky was able to soften the impact of that early bear market and not run out of money — a completely different story than if he had used a 5% W/D rate.

The results are much better, as you can see, but definitely not perfect. The 4% beginning W/D rate kept Mr. Unlucky from running out of money, but it's clear that he has one foot off the cliff. You might be wondering why this is, given he followed the research and used the recommended beginning W/D rate.

Good question.

Remember that the research behind the recommended beginning W/D rates is based on not running out of money. But we've set the bar higher than that — we're all about never *beginning* to run out of money.

So the beginning W/D rate is just that...a beginning. It's the first of two steps for protecting against unlucky fluctuation. It definitely reduces the impact of unlucky fluctuation, but it doesn't get rid of it altogether.

Summary

Withdrawal rates are your key to success when using the Rising Income Strategy. They help you start your retirement on the right path by establishing how much you can afford to pay yourself when you retire. Simply multiply your Nest Egg Value by the recommended beginning W/D rate for your age to determine the appropriate amount.

Using the right beginning W/D rate is your first step in protecting yourself against unlucky fluctuation. Your W/D rate is a powerful tool to use at the beginning of retirement, but you can also use it like a GPS to keep you on track as you continue along your retirement path.

Next Up: As you've seen, your beginning W/D rate alone doesn't prevent the possibility of never *beginning* to run out of money. For that, you need to learn how to keep your W/D rate at the right level throughout your retirement. That means learning to use your withdrawal rate to answer the question: *Am I in danger of running out of money in my retirement?*

Staying on the Right Path

As you've learned, unlucky fluctuation creates the possibility of running out of money in retirement...unless you have a plan to help protect against it.

Beginning your retirement with the right withdrawal rate helps, but it doesn't completely eliminate the chance of your running out of money. If unlucky fluctuation happens early enough and is severe enough, it has the power to send you off the cliff in a three-decade retirement. To fully protect against this, you need to know how much you can afford to pay yourself — not only at the beginning, but *during* your retirement too.

As each year goes by, your Rising Income Strategy is subject to fluctuation. Is it the kind of fluctuation that will cause you to begin running out of money? There's no way to know without checking. You need a way to measure the impact of fluctuation on your retirement savings. How else will you know if you're still on the right path, a safe distance from the cliff's edge?

> " What is your withdrawal rate **telling** you? Are you in danger of going **broke**? "

Once again, W/D rates come to the rescue — they can provide the answer.

Always There to Guide You

We said in the last chapter that W/D rates answer the two most important financial questions that every retiree has:

> 1. How much can I afford to pay myself when I retire?
> 2. Am I in danger of running out of money in my retirement?

In addition to starting your retirement off on the right path by answering the first question, W/D rates can tell you, each and every year, whether you're in danger of straying from this path. Remember, they're like a GPS for your RI Strategy. They have the power to assess the luckiness or unluckiness of the fluctuation that your Rising Income Strategy is experiencing. And they can suggest when you need a mid-course adjustment to keep you away from the cliff's edge.

Now, let's look at how W/D rates can help you answer our second question: *Am I in danger of running out of money in my retirement?*

Seeing the Full Picture

We've talked quite a bit about never beginning to run out of money. What we need now is a way to measure if this is actually happening. It's logical to think that the answer to this question is as simple as "Is my nest egg shrinking or not?" But this doesn't give you a full picture of what's going on with your RI Strategy — there's more to consider than just the current value of your retirement savings.

For starters, about every 4-5 years you may experience a bear market. This will temporarily decrease the value of your retirement savings. In addition, your life expectancy will be constantly changing. To top it all off, the cost of living will be increasing, requiring more income from your nest egg. You need to consider all these conditions to figure out if you've begun to run out of money.

Looking at two of our previous examples, you'll see that the value of a nest egg doesn't tell the whole story:

1. Ms. Lucky's nest egg *shrunk* nine times during her three-decade retirement while using a RI Strategy, and she turned out just fine. If your nest egg shrinks for one or two years in a row, it doesn't necessarily mean that you've begun to run out of money.

2. On the flip side, consider the LOI strategy, where the value of the hapless retiree's nest egg *never* shrunk. It stayed the same for the entire 30 years. But you probably also remember how well *that* worked out. The retiree's savings eventually fell behind the rising cost of living and sent him straight off the cliff. A nest egg value that *hasn't shrunk* doesn't mean you're not beginning to run out of money.

Staying on the Right Path

Nest egg values, number of years of retirement ahead, rising living costs…these all change. And you need to consider *all* of them to know if you're beginning to run out of money at any point in time during your retirement. W/D rates can help you do just that.

To stay safely on your retirement mountain, it's important that you answer this question accurately:

> Am I in danger of running out of money in my retirement?

Whenever a client asks me this question, my financial planner ears actually hear this:

> Am I still withdrawing at the right rate?

Just as there's the right W/D rate at the beginning of your retirement, there's also the right W/D rate at every stage *during* your retirement. These percentages are based on the same research that gave us the beginning W/D rates, but I've added my own bit of know-how for applying the best W/D rate to your RI Strategy.

Keeping your W/D rate at the right level is the second step in protecting yourself against unlucky fluctuation.

Tornado Warning

Growing up in Oklahoma, I learned about tornados at an early age. I also learned that there's a real difference between what the weatherman called a Tornado Watch and a Tornado Warning. When I was a kid, a Watch meant that Mom wouldn't get mad if we went outside to scan the sky for funnel clouds, as long as we stayed close to the house. A Warning meant that we should grab the dog and jump in the bathtub with pillows over our heads if we heard the sound of a freight train coming down the tracks... especially since there weren't train tracks anywhere near our house.

Tornado Warnings in Oklahoma are very real and very scary. Just 30 miles from where I grew up is a large college-like campus called the National Weather Service. The meteorologists and weather scientists at the NWS were the first in the country to use Doppler radar. They've always provided the most advanced weather forecasting in the country. All of us in Oklahoma were thankful to have them close by, watching out for us. And when they issued a Tornado Warning, we listened. It was serious business.

I guess those early lessons never left me, because even though I now live in a part of the country where tornados rarely pose a threat, I still have a weather radio next to my bed. I never miss a weather alert.

The National Weather Service has very clear definitions of a Tornado Watch and a Tornado Warning[1]:

- A *WATCH* is used when "the risk of a hazardous weather event has increased significantly, but its occurrence, location, or timing is still uncertain. It is intended to provide enough lead time so those who need to set their plans in motion can do so."

- A *WARNING* is issued when "a hazardous weather event is occurring, imminent, or likely. A warning means weather conditions pose a threat to life or property. People in the path of the storm need to take protective action."

Cow named Bossie who survived deadly 1947 tornado
Who doesn't love surfing the World Wide Web? That's where you'll find a photo of a cow named Bossie who supposedly survived the deadly 1947 tornado that swept a 221-mile path of destruction across Texas, Oklahoma, and Kansas.

Wouldn't it be cool if we had Watches and Warnings for our retirement withdrawal strategies? In the case of a Rate Watch, wouldn't it be great to know that the risk of running out of money had "increased, but was still uncertain," giving us enough lead time to "set our plans accordingly"? Or how about getting a Rate Warning when running out of money was "imminent or likely," giving us the information we'd need to "take protective action"?

Guess what? We do have a system like this...because I created one! In deference to those great people at the NWS, I call it the *W/D Rate Alert System*.

Think of it as the *You're Too Close to the Cliff! Alert System* or the *You're Going Broke! Alert System*.

Logic says that if you can identify the right beginning W/D rate based upon your age, you can also identify the right W/D rate *as you age*. With that in mind, I created the W/D Rate Alert System:

W/D Rate Alert System

Age	Recommended Beginning W/D Rate	Watch Zone (1 in 3)	Warning Zone (1 in 2)
50-59	3.5%	4% - 4.5%	> 4.5%
60-69	4%	4.5% - 5%	> 5%
70-79	5%	5.5% - 6.5%	> 6.5%
80+	6.5%	7% - 8%	> 8%

The W/D rate Watch and Warning Zones are based on the probability that unlucky fluctuation will cause you to run out of money. I'll spare you the mathematical details[2]. You just need to know that if your W/D rate is in the Watch Zone, you have a 1 in 3 chance of running out of money if you live to your normal life expectancy. The Warning Zone is a worse place to be — your chance of running out of money *there* is 1 in 2.

Yikes, better get ready to grab the dog and high-tail it to the bathtub!

Don't worry, I have a strategy for keeping your RI Strategy out of the Watch or Warning Zones. But first, let's figure out how to apply the W/D Rate Alert System.

Watching cows' behaviors to predict weather
As any old-time farmer knows, you just need to watch the cows to predict the weather. Folklore has it that when the herd spreads itself out in the field, there's clear weather ahead. The closer cows cluster, the worse the forecast. Signs of an approaching storm include restless cows that don't give milk, cows licking their forefeet, and a herd of cows lying down in the pasture.

The W/D Rate Alert System in Practice
I created the W/D Rate Alert System so that you could gauge the health of your Rising Income Strategy during your retirement. If your goal is to never begin running out of money in retirement, then you need to know exactly where you stand at any given point on your retirement path. The W/D Rate Alert System is designed to tell you if you're getting dangerously close to the edge of the cliff.

W/D rate alerts can provide valuable insights related to the luckiness or unluckiness of the fluctuation your RI Strategy is experiencing. More importantly, they can foreshadow a problem with your retirement plan — a problem like *beginning to run out of money*.

Let's revisit Ms. Lucky and Mr. Unlucky. The W/D Rate Alert System helps us see their situations in a more complete and constructive way. Instead of looking at the value of their nest eggs (which we know is a misleading measure of whether they've begun to run out of money), let's look at their W/D rates over time.

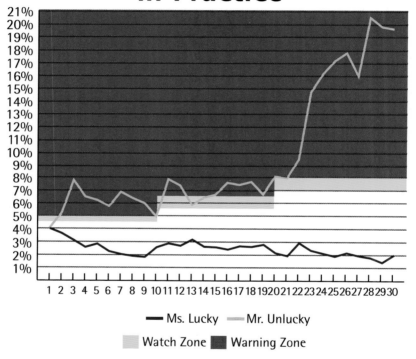

W/D Rate Alert System in Practice

Using the W/D Rate Alert System, we see some clues very early in Mr. Unlucky's retirement that things aren't going his way. Take a look at his first decade. In eight of those years, his W/D rate is either in the Watch or Warning Zone. That tells us that the risk of Mr. U beginning to run out of money has "increased significantly." By looking only at the value of his nest egg, we wouldn't know this.

Mr. Unlucky's second decade shows a similar trend. His W/D rate spent all ten years in the Watch and Warning Zones. In fact, eight of those years were in the Warning Zone. So it shouldn't have been a surprise that his W/D rate skyrocketed in the third decade. He was beginning to run out money. His W/D rate had been telling him for years that this time was coming. If only he'd had access to the W/D Rate Alert System. He would have realized he needed to make a mid-course correction that would have kept him on the right path. Just think — the W/D Rate Alert System could have saved him from going off the cliff!

Compare his orange line on the chart to Ms. Lucky's blue line and you can see why she succeeded and Mr. Unlucky didn't. Her lucky fluctuation — not running into an early bear market — meant she never entered the Watch Zone during the entire three decades of her retirement.

So what can we learn from these examples? Well, it's clear that a string of high W/D rates — those that raise alerts — can spell trouble later. They should never be ignored. They will almost always lead to unsustainable W/D rates later in retirement.

Okay, what do I mean by "unsustainable" W/D rates?

These are rates that are too high to support your Rising Income Strategy. If your W/D rate is too high, your G&I portfolio isn't able to earn enough each year to pay you an income *and* leave money to reinvest. An even higher rate means that your G&I portfolio can't earn enough to pay you an income without also depleting your nest egg. And that's when the downward fall of running out of money begins.

W/D Rates Matter

To avoid beginning to run out of money, you must do one thing — earn more than you spend. In Mr. Unlucky's case, this became an insurmountable challenge in his third decade. And this is why he began to run out of money.

Looking at his W/D rate in the third decade, we can see that it was solidly in the Warning Zone. By mid-decade, his W/D rate was over 16%. This meant that his G&I portfolio would have to earn at least 16% for Mr. Unlucky to avoid spending his principal. And it would have to do this each and every year.

Pretty unlikely, Mr. Unlucky.

Looks like the only hope for not going broke would be for Mr. Unlucky to not live beyond his normal life expectancy.

Not exactly an inspiring way to live, is it?

W/D rates that are too high to sustain always create financial hardship in retirement. They eventually force you down one of two paths. Either you continue to pay yourself a rising income and enter a spend down mode, or you cut your income to get your W/D rate back into the recommended zone. For example, Mr. Unlucky would have to take a *50% pay cut* to get back down to his recommended W/D rate in the third decade.

These are tough choices to have to make during your "golden years."

But this didn't have to happen to Mr. Unlucky...and it *doesn't have to* happen to you. You have the tools you need to recognize and protect against unlucky fluctuation. Using a Recommended Beginning W/D Rate, along with the W/D Rate Alert System, you'll know how to stay on the right path.

What if You Enter The Watch or Warning Zone?

Not all of us will be as lucky as Ms. Lucky in our retirement. More than likely, your W/D rate will enter the Watch or Warning Zone at some point during your three decades. But remember, these zones are just an alert, not proof positive that you're beginning to run out of money. So don't panic.

Having your W/D rate spend a year or two in the Watch or Warning Zone isn't enough to call for immediate action. Any bear market can push your withdrawal rate higher and trigger an alert, but often a bull market soon brings it back down into the recommended zone again. What you need to watch out for is a trend.

If you see that your W/D rate isn't recovering — that is, returning to your recommended rate — during a bull market, this is a trend that signals it's time to make an adjustment in your W/D rate. An "adjustment," of course, is another word for a pay cut. Consider paying yourself a little less to get your withdrawal rate back into the recommended zone. Little adjustments early in your retirement can prevent large pay cuts later in retirement.

Bear markets are always responsible for starting these trends. This is exactly what happened to Mr. Unlucky. His W/D rate never fully recovered from that early bear market; it stayed pretty much in the Watch and Warning Zones. Remember, unsustainable W/D rates mean you are at risk of beginning to run out of money. If you see this trend happening to you, it's time for you to make adjustments.

Adjustments — or pay cuts — aren't much fun, no matter how old you are. But this is a small price to pay for maintaining your retirement stability. It is the surest way to have confidence that you won't begin running out of money.

The truth is, W/D rates matter. And by making adjustments to keep your W/D rate within the recommended zone, you can prevent unlucky fluctuation from causing you to run out of money.

Summary

The two steps for protecting against unlucky fluctuation are:
1. Start retirement with the right W/D rate.
2. During retirement, keep your W/D rate at the right level (out of the Watch or Warning Zones).

Withdrawal rates help you answer the question: *Am I in danger of running out of money in my retirement?* Your W/D rate is your ever-present guide while implementing a Rising Income strategy.

If your W/D rate is too high to sustain, you can make adjustments to keep it within the recommended zone. Keeping your W/D at the right level is the second step in protecting yourself against unlucky fluctuation. It will help you stay on a safe path throughout your retirement.

Next up: Maybe right now you're thinking something like this:

"As useful as all this information is, it still doesn't make me feel very comfortable with using the Rising Income Strategy. I know I need to protect myself against unlucky fluctuation, but I don't like the idea of pay cuts. I mean, who wants to start making big sacrifices in spending just because the stock market is down?"

"I know that the RI Strategy is the only one that can keep up with three decades of rising living costs. I just wish there were some way that my income could be more predictable."

If you're thinking any variation of the statements above, I have good news for you. In the next chapter, we'll look at a plan I've created for getting rid of all this uncertainty. Best of all, there are no pay cuts during your retirement.

Taking Control of Your Financial Destiny

Congratulations for getting this far. You've learned how to create an effective withdrawal strategy that protects you against unlucky fluctuation in retirement.

- You have a strategy for paying yourself an income for 30 years.

- You have a strategy for keeping up with living costs that will double.

- You have a tool to start you off on the right path and keep you there, happy on your retirement mountain, throughout your retirement.

There's only one thing missing. You don't have the confidence that there won't be pay cuts on the path ahead.

But that's about to change.

Time to Take Control

The only factor that causes a Rising Income Strategy to begin running out of money is

> **"You don't have to take pay cuts."**

unlucky fluctuation — a market decline. You just learned how to protect against unlucky fluctuation with a powerful tool — your Withdrawal Rate — but that may mean taking a pay cut at some point during your retirement.

Wouldn't it be great if we could do better than *protect against* unlucky fluctuation? Wouldn't it be great if we could make unlucky fluctuation a non-factor? In other words, wouldn't it be great to take control of your financial destiny in retirement?

Controlling your own financial destiny in retirement involves wrestling back the control that unlucky fluctuation has over you. And there's actually a simple move you can use to get on top of unlucky fluctuation and limit its power against you.

Your Counter Move against Unlucky Fluctuation (UF)

As any good wrestler knows, the opening move often makes or breaks the match. UF can gain the advantage by hitting you with an early bear market. This creates a tremendous amount of early stress on your RI Strategy. It forces you to use a higher W/D rate, keeping you from having money left over to reinvest. No money to reinvest means no chance to use the power of compounding.

UF's opening move is a tough one — it may tilt the odds against you long-term. If unlucky fluctuation's move is strong enough, you may never fully recover from it.

Don't let unlucky fluctuation gain the advantage! What you need to win the match against UF is a really good counter move. And once you learn to use it, you can prevent unlucky fluctuation from controlling your financial destiny.

The unusual Swiss tradition of cow wrestling

Believe it or not, cow wrestling is a traditional event in the Swiss Alps. This isn't like bullfighting — it's strictly cow versus cow, and according to online reports, there's no bloodshed. The sport calls for a special breed of cow naturally inclined to fight for dominance within the herd. Farmers and spectators cheer as the cows lock blunted horns for a pushing and shoving contest in the ring. And naturally, there are wages on the winner.

The Down Market Counter Move

When you're on the mat, this counter move makes all the difference. The very first time that UF throws a market decline at you, be prepared to meet that move with a powerful one of your own. And remember, we're not talking pay cuts here.

Let this simple counter move put you back on top...and in control:

Down Market Counter Move
Don't take a pay raise the year after you experience a down market.

Unlucky fluctuation expects you to take a pay raise like you do each and every year. But during a down market, pay raises create a double stress — an increased withdrawal that cuts into your principal plus a decreasing nest egg value. This double stress gives UF the power to push your W/D rate into a Watch or Warning Zone and keep it there for a long time…maybe forever. But only if you let it. To keep UF from gaining the advantage, you need to take away the pay raise.

You don't need to take a pay *cut*, just don't take a pay *raise* the year after you experience a down market. Keep your income exactly the same by taking out the same *dollar amount* you took the year before. This is a powerful counter move to prevent UF from taking control. I call it the Down Market Counter Move (DMCM).

It seems too simple, doesn't it? Trust me, a DMCM will beat UF every time. Let me show you just how well it works, and then we'll discuss exactly *why* it works.

Mr. Unlucky vs. Unlucky Fluctuation...THE REMATCH!

You remember Mr. Unlucky, right? He got clobbered by unlucky fluctuation back in Chapter 8, but it's a brand new chapter now. Mr. Unlucky is back for a rematch with his old rival — UF.

Mr. Unlucky's got a bold new attitude and a bold new counter move to go with it. He announces:

"I won't take a pay raise the year after I experience a down market."

Let's listen in on his pre-rematch interview:

Mr. Unlucky: *"My strategy is simple. If there's a market decline, I'll hold my annual withdrawal to the same dollar amount that it was the year before. I won't pay myself any less than I did the year before; I just won't pay myself more.*

"Once the market gives me a positive return, I'll start giving myself pay raises of 3.5% again. It doesn't even matter if the market

isn't fully recovered from the down market — as long as I have a positive return, I'll go back to my pay raises."

Interviewer: *"What if you have two down market years in a row?"*

Mr. Unlucky: *"No problem. I'll keep my pay the same for two years in a row. I've already worked out my strategy, based on what happened during my first match with UF in Chapter 8. Want to see it?"*

Interviewer: *"Sure, but aren't you worried that UF might see it?"*

Mr. Unlucky: *"Nah. Doesn't matter — there's nothing UF can do about it. He's lost the match before we even start. I'll be in control of my financial destiny, no matter what he throws at me.*

"Check it out. This time I'll meet his moves with my own counter moves.

"So, if UF tries the same move he used the last time — an early bear market during the first two years of my retirement — I'm ready for him. The year after each negative return, I'll just keep my income the same.

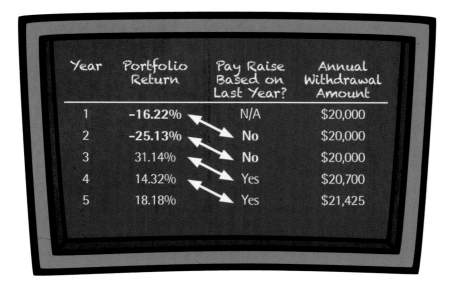

Year	Portfolio Return	Pay Raise Based on Last Year?	Annual Withdrawal Amount
1	-16.22%	N/A	$20,000
2	-25.13%	No	$20,000
3	31.14%	No	$20,000
4	14.32%	Yes	$20,700
5	18.18%	Yes	$21,425

"Look at the nasty move UF pulled in the first and second year of my retirement. He might try that again. If he does, I won't get my first pay raise until the fourth year of my retirement. That's because I only take a pay raise the year after a positive investment return.

"And hey, it's a small sacrifice, considering. Just wait until you see how easily I take UF down this time around."

Mr. Unlucky Wins Rematch!

As expected, UF tried the same bear market moves that he used on Mr. Unlucky back in Chapter 8. Mr. Unlucky was faced with the same set of returns that caused him to begin running out of money last time around. But Mr. Unlucky was right — he *was* ready for this rematch. Using the Down Market Counter Move, Mr. Unlucky immediately got on top of UF and took back control of his financial destiny.

Takedown! His W/D rate tells the story:

Mr. Unlucky's W/D Rate Alerts The Rematch!

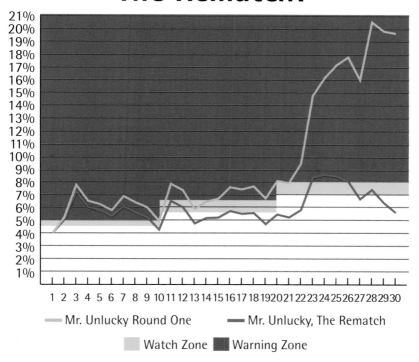

Mr. Unlucky Round One   Mr. Unlucky, The Rematch

Watch Zone   Warning Zone

Wow, what a difference! You can see that, using the DMCM, Mr. Unlucky's W/D rate was in the Watch and Warning Zones far less over time, minimizing his Rate Alerts. No wonder Mr. Unlucky felt confident this time around. Using his counter move, he never began running out of money.

What Price Glory?

Clearly, Mr. Unlucky emerged the victor in this rematch with UF, but at what price? Keeping his W/D rate at the right level came at a cost, didn't it? Even if he never had to take a pay cut, he did forgo some pay raises along the way. Wasn't he paying himself less overall?

The short answer…yes.

In this example, Mr. Lucky didn't get a pay raise during nine of his 30 retirement years. The question is, considering the impact of compounding, did he manage to keep up with the rising cost of living after forgoing these pay raises?

Let's take a look:

Mr. Unlucky's Income with Down Market Counter Move

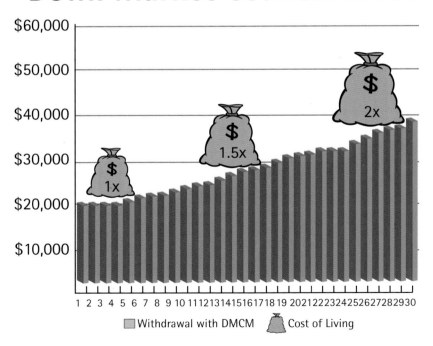

Mr. Unlucky's income was 1.5x his first year's budget when he reached the 18th year of his retirement; it was about 2x his first year's budget when he reached the 30th year. He hit the targets later in each decade, but he hit them.

It's true that he didn't increase his yearly income as fast as he would have if he didn't use the Down Market Counter Move. But it's also true that his small sacrifices along the way kept his W/D rate in the recommended zone for the majority of his retirement, which created prosperous results. Mr. Unlucky was never faced with having to make a big lifestyle adjustment later in life to avoid falling off the cliff. Just look at the value of his Nest Egg with and without the DMCM:

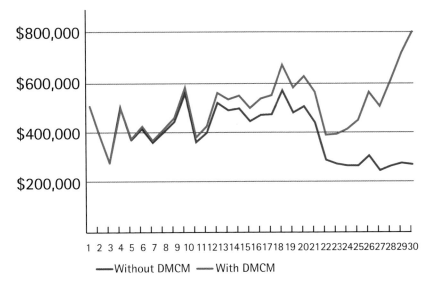

Mr. Unlucky's Nest Egg Values

Something amazing happened in that third decade. Not only was Mr. Unlucky *not* beginning to run out of money, he actually *increased* the value of his nest egg. He had about $500,000 more in Year 30 using the Down Market Counter Move than he would have had without it.

The Financial Scoop

MR. UNLUCKY VICTORIOUS!

Considering name change...

That's $500,000 more earning power, $500,000 more flexibility, and 500,000 more reasons to sleep well at night. That's powerful…and all it took was small adjustments (a few years without pay raises) along the way to avoid a big lifestyle shock later.

1…2…3…Mr. Unlucky wins! UF is officially a NF (as in Non-Factor)!

Why the Down Market Counter Move Works

There are three explanations for why the DMCM works. One has to do with lifestyle, one has to do with psychology, and one has to do with math.

> 1. Let's start with the lifestyle explanation.

It's human nature to develop a comfort level with the financial means and lifestyle you're used to, particularly in retirement. A pay cut — especially an unexpected pay cut — is disruptive and unsettling. Most people would agree that keeping their pay the same is easier to deal with than taking an unexpected pay cut. The beauty of the Down Market Counter Move is that it's lifestyle-friendly. It will never ask you to take a pay cut. And there's peace of mind in knowing that.

Remember the Holy Cow Moment in Chapter 4, that all-night fretting about whether or not the money saved would be enough? Racing, fear-driven thoughts are typical symptoms. The HCM is known to hit both men and women at various stages in their retirements. If there's a retiree out there who hasn't yet experienced the Holy Cow Moment, you will. Just wait for your first market decline.

I've had to calm down plenty of nervous clients during bear markets. Nobody feels good in the middle of one. In extreme cases, people panic. They feel like they need to do *something...anything* to avoid running out of money. They worry that this time the market really *won't* recover, even though it always has in the past. The impulse to do *something* can have terrible long-term effects. Think of retirees who sell their G&I portfolios and then put everything into a savings account. They lock in the decreased value of their nest eggs and run the risk that they will miss the market recovery.

The psychological good news is that the Down Market Counter Move does indeed let you do something. By not giving yourself a pay raise, you've done something to take back control. I can't overstate the importance of feeling some control during a market decline. It's the sense of powerlessness that causes many people to make poor investment choices during these times.

I know that the DMCM won't calm your nerves completely, but it will keep you in charge of your finances. And there's a very good chance that it'll reduce the strength and duration of your Holy Cow Moments.

Here's the secret behind why the DMCM works: By forgoing pay raises periodically, you're actually paying yourself less overall during your retirement. You could also say that by paying yourself less overall, you're putting less stress on your nest egg.

Take a look at the annual income that Mr. Unlucky was withdrawing from his nest egg in the 15th year of his retirement — both with and without the Down Market Counter Move:

■ With the Down Market Counter Move: $28,212

■ Without the Down Market Counter Move: $32,374

Mr. Unlucky was paying himself nearly 13% less with this strategy at the midpoint of his retirement. This meant 13% less stress on his nest egg — not only that year, but every year thereafter. The Down Market Counter Move may be annual in its implementation, but it is lifelong in its impact. It's like a gift that keeps on giving.

The pay raise you forgo keeps fighting against unlucky fluctuation long after you've resumed your pay increases. Once you do the math, it's easy to see that this counter move keeps UF from ever gaining the advantage.

Someone At The Social Security
Administration Has Figured This Out

Soon after I developed the Down Market Counter Move, I searched the financial planning world to see if anyone else had discovered this simple and effective solution. Nobody had. But then I saw a news story that confirmed I wasn't the only one who knew the power of the math behind this strategy. The headline read:
No Social Security Increase for Seniors for Second Year in a Row.[1]

To quiet the impending uproar, they offered seniors a one-time $250 payment to offset the lack of a pay increase.

It took me only a minute to realize what this meant for the future of the Social Security "lockbox", which is the equivalent of your nest egg. It meant that Social Security would be paying out much less over time than it would have if it continued to offer a pay increase. The Social Security system essentially eliminated two years of compounding. This will reduce future payouts by billions of dollars. I suspect someone over at the Social Security office figured out the same math I have; they just aren't telling anybody.

As for the $250 one-time payment? This was a way to provide seniors with an income that wouldn't be included in compounding calculations to determine social security payouts years down the road. That means the Social Security system will be paying out less in benefits.

Very clever...or sneaky, depending on your perspective.

Summary

A successful retirement depends on financial confidence. The recommended way to achieve this is by making unlucky fluctuation a non-factor.

The Down Market Counter Move is the simple act of forgoing a pay raise the year after you experience a down market. It's your way of taking control of your financial destiny so that you never venture close to the cliff's edge. The Down Market Counter Move is easy to implement and it works. It gives you the confidence that you'll never begin running out of money in retirement.

Deep inhale...now, exhale. Doesn't that feel better? It's time to go enjoy your retirement.

Next Up: We'll put all that you've learned together through a couple of examples that apply the book's lessons to real life situations. You'll meet one couple just setting out on the retirement path. And you'll meet another couple in mid-retirement who needs a course correction.

Putting it All Together

Let's put everything you now know about creating and implementing a Rising Income Strategy into practice. At the very beginning of this book, I told you that I realized that I didn't need to become a better salesman; I needed to become a better storyteller. Since stories are often the best way to learn, I'm sharing a couple of stories from my own financial planning practice to show you how your new knowledge about a financially successful retirement can be applied in the real world.

I've chosen two examples that are typical of the many retirement income planning meetings I've had in my career. The first couple is just arriving at retirement and creating their first withdrawal strategy. The second couple is ten years into retirement and has concerns about their current withdrawal strategy.

You may find this chapter a little nerdy and it has a bit of math. But think of it like Reality TV — there's a lesson or two that makes it worthwhile. And if you're not really sure how all the components, like Social Security,

> **"**Choosing to **never run out** of money = **confidence**. What's that worth? **"**

155

a pension, etc., that factor into a retirement's financial "picture" come together, you'll find it valuable.

Meet Russ and Wendy — New Retirees

Russ and Wendy will be retiring at the end of the year, and they couldn't be happier. They're at the beginning stage of putting a plan in place for taking an income from their nest egg. Their kids are out of college, married, and starting their own families. Russ and Wendy are looking forward to spending time with their two new grandchildren, doing a bit of traveling, and sipping their morning coffee without feeling rushed. They know that to fully enjoy all of these things, they need a plan that gives them the confidence that they'll never begin to run out of money. They want to always feel as financially stable as they do today.

You're invited to join my meeting with Russ and Wendy to check out how the process goes.

They tell me that they want the following:

- A plan that will make their money last as long as they do...no matter how many years that is.
- A plan that can keep up when things start costing more in the future.
- A plan that will prevent them from becoming a burden to their children.

Russ sums things up for me: "We're not interested in getting rich, Chuck. We just don't want to become poor in retirement."

I smile. "There's a withdrawal strategy for that," I say.

Okay, so here's a question for *you*: What did Russ and Wendy just ask me for?

That's right — they need the Rising Income Strategy.

I explain the two blind spots to Russ and Wendy. They aren't really surprised at how long they'll be living or how much more things will cost, but they *are* surprised by the magnitude of each of those challenges.

"Wow," Wendy says. "I'm not sure we can afford to retire yet."

"Yes, you can," I say, "if you have the right withdrawal strategy. Let's take a look at where you're at right now, and then I'll show you how we can put you on a safe path to where you're headed."

Just the Facts Ma'am

At retirement, Russ & Wendy have the following assets, sources of income, and budget.

Ages: Russ- 66, Wendy- 64

Annual Income Sources:
Social Security & Pensions: $54,000

Annual Expenses:
(1st Year Budget): $90,000

Retirement Savings Or Nest Egg Value (For Producing An Income):
401k's - $600,000
IRA's - $200,000

Cash Reserves (For The Unexpected):
Checking/Savings/Money Market Accounts: $100,000

There are a couple more important facts about Russ and Wendy that you should know before we get into the numbers. First, Wendy has always let Russ handle the investments. She worries about the stock market...in fact, she wants as much money as possible anywhere *but* the stock market. Second, Russ is comfortable with growth investing, but isn't clear how much he should be doing.

Since he will no longer be working, he says he doesn't "have the time to recover from a bad market like I used to."

With that in mind, we begin to create their withdrawal strategy. I show them the three strategies and they quickly realize that the Rising Income Strategy is the only one designed to make their money last for their lifetimes, even with the rising costs inflation is sure to bring.

The Simple Math: Determining the First-Year Withdrawal Amount

We take a close look at Russ and Wendy's first year budget. What we're really interested in is just how much income they'll need to get from their retirement savings each year. To find out, we subtract their current income sources from their budget:

$$\begin{aligned} &\$90,000 \text{ (First-Year Annual Budget)} \\ - \; &\$54,000 \text{ (Income Sources)} \\ \hline = \; &\$36,000 \text{ (Income Needed From Retirement Savings)} \end{aligned}$$

We see that Russ and Wendy would like to get $36,000 from their nest egg each year to supplement their other income. This will be their first-year Annual Withdrawal Amount (AWA). (Remember, with the RI Strategy, each year, unless there has been a down market, Wendy and Russ will give themselves a 3.5% raise.)

From this information, we can calculate their expected W/D rate. Let's apply our formula from Chapter 9:

$$\$36,000 \text{ (AWA)} \div \$800,000 \text{ (Nest Egg Value)} = 4.5\% \text{ W/D Rate}$$

Hmm...interesting. If you recall, the recommended W/D rate for a 64-year-old (we always use the youngest person's age) is 4%. So what if the budget is asking for more than 4%?

Well, it depends on how much more. Let's check out the Withdrawal Rate Alert System to see if it's sending us any alarms here:

W/D Rate Alert System

Age	Recommended Beginning W/D Rate	Watch Zone (1 in 3)	Warning Zone (1 in 2)
50-59	3.5%	4% - 4.5%	> 4.5%
60-69	4%	4.5% - 5%	> 5%
70-79	5%	5.5% - 6.5%	> 6.5%
80+	6.5%	7% - 8%	> 8%

For their age bracket, Russ and Wendy's planned W/D rate of 4.5% is higher than the Recommended Rate and actually just enters the lower end of the Watch Zone. Considering that Russ and Wendy are in their mid-60's, I consider a 4.5% beginning W/D rate okay. If they were a few years younger, I'd suggest that they adjust their budget to fit a 4% W/D rate.

Creating the Rising Income Strategy Investment Portfolio

After discussing the beginning W/D rate, our conversation turns to how to invest their retirement savings.

"Wow, all we have to do is earn the 4.5% that we're withdrawing and we won't ever run out of money." says Wendy. "That seems pretty easy."

"Not so fast," I say. "If all you earn is 4.5%, you have an LOI Strategy. You'll need to earn more than that to have a RI Strategy. Remember your blind spots."

"Oh yeah," Wendy says. "I forgot about inflation."

"Right," I say, as I grab my calculator. "Let's do the math."

By putting two pieces of information together — Russ and Wendy's W/D rate and the inflation rate — we determine how much their nest egg will need to earn. This is useful information for designing an investment portfolio.

> 4.5% W/D Rate + 3.5% Inflation = 8% required growth rate

"Holy cow," says Russ. "Eight percent means a huge amount of growth for our portfolio."

Wendy immediately objects. "We can't afford to lose money in retirement. Isn't there a way we could have less in growth investments?"

"Sure, but it would require that you spend less," I say.

She grimaces. "How much less? How much income could we take if we put everything in guaranteed investments?"

Wendy is asking the right questions here. To create their Rising Income Strategy, we need to set it up so that they spend less than they earn. Their portfolio should be growing each and every year to keep pace with the rising cost of living.

To answer Wendy's question, I need to know what kind of guaranteed rate is available. In this case, I assume I can find something that will earn 5%, guaranteed...as in fixed, never to fluctuate.

It's easy to figure out how much they can spend if they choose this no-growth, all guaranteed portfolio. We simply subtract inflation from the 5% rate of growth...and that's Russ and Wendy's W/D rate.

5% Guaranteed Rate — 3.5% Inflation = 1.5% W/D Rate

This means:

1.5% W/D rate from a $800,000 nest egg = $12,000
Russ & Wendy's beginning annual withdrawal amount

Russ's reaction is immediate: "But that's not even close to the $36,000 we'd be getting from the G&I portfolio version of this plan!"

"Chuck, you've got to be kidding," says Wendy. "I thought you said that we could use either a fixed portfolio or growth portfolio plan with the Rising Income Strategy."

"You can, you can." I say, using my ever-patient financial advisor voice. "Both plans work and both are designed to do the same thing — keep up with the rising cost of living. But numbers don't lie."

Russ and Wendy sigh deeply, in unison.

I continue: "If you earn less, you have to take less — otherwise you're going off the cliff. You just can't take $36,000 out of a guaranteed, fixed income plan without running out of money in retirement."

The Dilemma

The dilemma facing Russ and Wendy is one that most retirees face: finding a balance between getting the income that they want and owning as few fluctuating investments as possible.

This is really the heart of the retirement income challenge for many of today's retirees. They've saved just enough money to retire with a recommended withdrawal rate. However, to keep up with three decades of rising living costs, the largest part of their portfolio must be in growth investments. Most retirees would prefer to have as few growth investments — subject to fluctuation — as possible.

It sounds odd, but it's possible that the more conservative your investment portfolio is, the more likely it is that you'll run out of money in retirement. In Russ and Wendy's case, they can't take a 4.5% withdrawal and keep up with 3.5% inflation if they're only earning 4.5% on their retirement savings. If they do this, they are on the path to going broke in retirement.

But let's take a look at the other side of this dilemma.

The lower your W/D rate, the more conservative your portfolio can be. In other words, the more money you have to begin with, the more conservative you can afford to be. For Russ and Wendy to generate $36,000 from a 5% guaranteed portfolio and still keep up with 3.5% inflation, they'd need to have $2,400,000 in their nest egg.

> $2,400,000 x 1.5% W/D rate = $36,000 annual withdrawal

"Yikes. We don't have anywhere near that much," says Wendy.

Russ is shaking his head. "I thought I was doing a pretty good job with our investments, but these numbers…"

I quickly reassure them both: "You're not alone — most retirees find themselves in your position. Not many people have enough in their retirement savings to be able to live on a 1.5% withdrawal rate."

"You're saying I can't afford to be as conservative as I'd like to be, right, Chuck?" asks Wendy.

"I can't change the numbers," I say gently. "You're going to have to own a growth portfolio in some form."

Russ reminds me, "We're not interested in getting rich, Chuck. We just don't want to become poor in retirement."

"I know, Russ," I say. "I know."

Nobody says that succeeding in a three-decade, rising living cost retirement with a G&I portfolio is effortless. It requires discipline and knowledge to start off on the right path and then stay on it. You can't wing it.

Russ & Wendy's Rising Income Strategy

After our meeting, Russ and Wendy decide to get more serious about their retirement budget. They realize that they had padded it quite a bit and see a few areas where it's unrealistic and excessive.

They call me for a second meeting.

When we sit down together again, they decide that a $24,000 beginning annual withdrawal amount will meet their needs. This means a W/D rate of only 3%. When we add our 3.5% inflation rate, this means that their required portfolio growth target is 6.5%.

This allows me to create a more conservative portfolio, combining both growth and fixed accounts, that lets Wendy sleep at night and gives them both the confidence that they'll be able to keep up with inflation and make their money last for their lifetimes.

Success.

Meet Harry and Evelyn — Nervous Retirees

Harry and Evelyn had already been retired for ten years when we first met. Both had retired at the age of 62 from careers that they enjoyed. But both admitted that they were enjoying retirement even more.

Evelyn left the school system after a 35-year teaching career. She missed the kids, but not the politics that had consumed her job the last few years before she left. Harry was a retired engineer for a textile company. When his company started moving jobs overseas, they offered him an early retirement package. They didn't have to ask him twice.

During the first ten years of their retirement, Harry and Evelyn fulfilled a couple of lifelong dreams. The year after they retired, they spent two unhurried months sightseeing in Europe and ended the trip with a Mediterranean cruise. A couple of years after that, they organized and sponsored a family reunion, which consisted of a two-week trip to Alaska. Their two children brought their spouses and all five of Harry and Evelyn's grandchildren for an unforgettable vacation. It was, Harry said, one of the most wonderful times of his life.

Closer to home, Evelyn put now-retired Harry to work on her honey-do list. She had always wanted to have the kitchen and bathroom remodeled. About one week into the job, Harry realized it was beyond his skill level, so he called in the contractors. One thing led to another, and the remodeling project grew. The kitchen was enlarged by moving the back wall of the house out 15 feet. This allowed them to add a sunroom, where they enjoy breakfast together every morning.

Harry and Evelyn's remodeling project had been completed for about six months at the time I sat down with them in my office.

Harry began the conversation:

"When we retired ten years ago, we had a retirement plan done for us. Because of our pensions, our advisor said we were in great shape for retirement. And, Chuck, we had about $1.5 million in retirement savings to cover the income shortfall that wasn't covered by our pensions and social security. We thought we were golden. And these were going to be our 'golden' years. Get it?

"Anyhow, in the beginning, we were only taking about $50,000 from our savings to pay for the trips and other expenses. We kept pretty good records of what we were spending for the first couple of years. The market was good to us. Even though we began taking a little more than the $50,000 a few years later, our $1.5 million savings stayed the same. So we figured we were okay."

Can you say LOI mindset? I thought to myself. But I kept quiet.

"Now, 10 years later, after this money pit of a remodeling project and two years in a row of a crummy stock market, our retirement savings is only worth $900,000. The last two years, we've taken out about $70,000 to pay for stuff we needed."

At this point, Evelyn chimed in:

"We're worried, Chuck. We're afraid that we're spending too much and that our retirement savings won't be able to grow fast enough to keep up. We're hoping you can help us understand what we should be spending so that we don't begin to lose our principal."

I'm Glad You Asked

I assured Harry and Evelyn that they'd come to the right place. I spent some time going through the information in this book and then showed them their W/D rate:

$$\$70,000 \div \$900,000 = 7.77\%$$

Just then, Harry glanced at the *W/D Rate Alert System* chart on my desk and said, "Uh oh."

"Uh oh" was right. The recommended W/D rate for Harry and Evelyn at age 72 is 5%. At the 7.77% W/D rate that they were taking, they stood a better than 1 in 2 chance of running out of money if they lived to their normal life expectancies. I tried to help them understand how serious their situation was:

"At the rate of $70,000/year, you've already begun to run out of money. You have one foot off the cliff. It's time to put you back on solid ground. But it's going to require an adjustment to your income.

"Let's talk about your withdrawal rate in the context of current market conditions. Since we've seen a bear market for the last two

years, most investors' withdrawal rates are edging closer to the Watch and Warning Zones. We know that history repeats itself, right? This means that the next bull market, whenever it comes, will help improve withdrawal rates without any change in the amount of income you're taking.

"But in your case, I don't think that bull market will be enough to get you back on track. You're going to need to be proactive. You've got to make an adjustment to your withdrawals to get back the confidence you had in your financial future at the beginning of your retirement.

"To put your plan back on track, I suggest you reduce your annual withdrawal to at least the lower end of the Watch Zone — that's 5.5%. If you can do more, then do more. But at 5.5%, your income will be about $50,000 instead of $70,000. I know this is a hefty pay cut, but it's the only way to pull yourself back from the cliff's edge.

"And I'd also suggest you forgo any kind of pay raise until your withdrawal rate gets back into the recommended zone. From that point forward, we'll use the Down Market Counter Move to keep you on a safe path."

How did Harry and Evelyn take this news? Well, they weren't happy, but Evelyn said that there were places where she knew they could cut back. But then Harry had a question:

"Chuck, can we avoid taking such a drastic cut back? What if we just dropped our withdrawal to $60,000?"

Hey, you can't blame a guy for trying, I thought. But I had to tell it to them straight:

"At $60,000, that means your withdrawal rate would be 6.7%. That's well into the Warning Zone. You've still got a better than 50/50 chance that you'll run out of money.

"It's your money; you can do what you want. But you came here for my advice...and this is it: Don't go broke in retirement. These are your golden years — you don't want to spend them worrying. Think of it this way: You're not making a choice to cut back; you're making a choice to never run out of money. We're talking about your financial stability here. Now, what's that worth?"

Harry and Evelyn looked at each other for a moment, and then they both agreed that they needed to make the adjustments I suggested. Harry admitted that they should have paid closer attention to how their spending decisions over the last ten years would impact their overall plan. Evelyn patted his hand and told him not to dwell on the past — it was time to concentrate on regaining control of their financial future.

So, any prospective trips to Europe for Harry and Evelyn have been delayed for a while. But at least they have that nice sunroom to enjoy while they plan their way back to a financially confident retirement.

Summary

Smart retirement income planning is a process that never stops. No matter where you are on your retirement journey — just starting out or somewhere along your path — you can use the tools and strategies you've learned in this book to guide you.

Oh...one more thing. Don't do this alone.

Next Up: Your retirement is too important to leave to chance. You don't have the option of learning from your mistakes and starting over. For financial success in your golden years, you need to get retirement right from the very beginning. You need a guide who can identify potential mistakes and oversights long before they send you over the cliff.

Don't Go It Alone

What makes a professional a professional?

About 10,000 hours of practice, according to Malcolm Gladwell, author of the fascinating book *Outliers*. Gladwell makes the case that becoming truly proficient at something — like playing the piano or solving math problems — isn't necessarily the result of having an inborn talent. Rather, it's directly related to the amount of time you practice a skill. Maybe this is what Einstein meant when he said, "It's not that I'm so smart, it's just that I stay with problems longer."

Just how long is 10,000 hours? Well, if you were to work a 40-hour week and take two weeks of vacation each year, it would take five full years to put in 10,000 hours. It would take a weekend warrior, who practices four hours each Saturday and Sunday, more than 24 years to put in 10,000 hours. The pay off for all of this practice? Being very good at what you do. Very, very good.

If you were an adventurous sort and decided that you wanted to climb Mt. Everest, you wouldn't choose to do so alone. You would hire

> " It's not that I'm so **smart**, it's just that I stay with problems **longer**. "
>
> ALBERT EINSTEIN

a guide — a professional. You'd want someone who has put in 10,000 hours of mountaineering and has been to the summit and back more than once. When planning a climb that you know can be treacherous, you want a guide who knows the mountain intimately. You want a guide who has thought through potential problems (that you didn't even know existed) and created contingency plans for them. A good guide's first duty is to guide you up and down the mountain safely. Because your guide has the ability to steer you away from trouble, your journey will be a more pleasant one.

Sure, it's possible to reach the summit of Mt. Everest and return safely without hiring a guide or putting in your own 10,000 hours of practice. But is it worth putting your life at risk like this? Hiring a professional guide not only greatly increases your chance of success, but also greatly reduces your chances of making a fatal mistake.

How is your retirement any different?

We've talked a lot about the retirement mountain. Choosing to retire is not all that different from choosing to climb Mount Everest. You're setting out on a journey that's filled with hidden challenges and treacherous paths. But it's the trip of a lifetime. And you have only one chance to get it right.

Do you plan to learn as you go, or would you prefer to have a guide — someone who has put in his or her 10,000 hours, knows the terrain, and can guide you safely throughout your journey? A good advisor can mean the difference between living a financially successful retirement and going right off the cliff.

The Right Guide

On a Sunday morning in May 2008, Min Bahadur Sherchan entered the world record books. At the age of 76, this Nepalese climber became the oldest person to reach the 29,035 foot summit of Mt. Everest...and return safely. [1]

Over 1,400 people have reached Everest's summit since Sir Edmund Hillary first accomplished this feat in 1953. But anyone who attempts to scale this highest peak on earth knows that more than 200 people have perished in their attempts. This is not a journey for the unprepared.

For his journey, Sherchan chose arguably the most accomplished and prepared guide on the mountain, Pemba Dorjee Sherpa. A world record holder himself, Pemba Dorjee Sherpa holds the record for the fastest summit of Mt. Everest. But speed wasn't the goal in this case. A successful summit was. And succeed they did.

Their success is a testament to both men's courage and initiative. More than that, it serves as an example of how the right guide can apply their knowledge and experience to help others meet challenges and achieve a level of success that they just could not on their own.

Two Ways an Advisor Helps You

A financially successful retirement doesn't happen by chance. It takes some work. A professional advisor can make this work easier and less time-consuming than you thought possible. The payoff of working with an advisor isn't just the time it saves you, it's the confidence it gives you, knowing you'll have an experienced guide with you along your retirement journey.

My job as a financial advisor is really very simple...not easy, but simple. For each retired client I serve, I must do two things:

- Start them off on the right path.
- Keep them on the right path.

Which brings us back to our falling cows one last time — those cows wouldn't have tumbled off their respective mountains if they'd never gotten close to the edge in the first place! Too bad they didn't have a guide to not only show them their blind spots, but to start them off and *keep* them on a path that led to green pastures instead of danger.

For retirees, starting off on the right path begins with a comprehensive plan — one that takes into consideration your complete financial picture. Your withdrawal strategy is created as part of this plan. We've covered a few examples in this book, but your financial situation probably isn't as simple as the examples presented here. Consider:

- Social Security will be a part of your income plan, but it won't be growing at 3.5% each year to keep up with inflation. This means that over time, your retirement savings will be picking up more of the tab for your income needs.

- You may have a pension from your employer. Will the pension payments last for your entire life? How about your spouse's life if you pass first? Does the payment increase each year? If so, by how much?

- Your income needs may change significantly during retirement. For example: Is your house paid for or will you be paying it off during your retirement? Are you receiving funds from a business sale or legal settlement? What if one of the kids moves back?! What if you or your spouse require long-term care?

■ Your tax situation may change. Did you factor that into your annual budget, or will that consume part of the amount you will be withdrawing from your retirement savings each year. Will you be in a lower or higher tax bracket as you progress through retirement?

This is the kind of stuff that takes sophisticated computer software to figure out. And let me tell you, the training required to run a program like this is the equivalent of a college course. But it's just one small part of a financial advisor's 10,000 hours.

Using the financial industry's best training and tools, a trusted advisor can create a beautiful Rising Income Strategy that will set you off on the right path in retirement. After that, your advisor continues to guide you so that you never stray from it.

Keeping You on the Right Path — The Real Challenge

Do you know the biggest enemy of smart investing? Emotion. Fear and greed have ruined many fortunes in the investment world. With retirees, I've found fear to be the dominant emotion. Remember what Russ said in the last chapter?

"We're not interested in getting rich, Chuck. We just don't want to become poor in retirement."

Greed is clearly not the emotion I have to worry about with Russ — it's fear.

Fear is the number one reason retirees stray from their safe path. The first

SURPRISE!

bear market they meet in retirement becomes a near end-of-the-world experience for them. This emotion is more powerful than reason. Retirees seem to completely forget the promise of the successful future that their RI strategy has in store for them. It's my job to help them overcome their fear and keep them safely on their path.

In the context of my relationship with my clients, this means keeping their faith in the plan we've created. It means giving them the confidence that they are on the right path...even though the markets may be trying to convince them otherwise. It's my job to be a voice of reason when the markets have caused a retiree to throw reason out the window.

The ideas laid out in this book are part of my "keep the faith" mission. It's much easier to have faith in the future when you've seen how the decisions you make along the way will impact it. I hope that what you've read will help you keep the faith in times of uncertainty.

One Last Thought

During the course of our focus groups, I asked my clients why they chose to work with an advisor instead of creating their retirement income strategy themselves. Here's what they had to say:

"I just don't feel like I know enough about investing to do this myself."

"I feel better knowing someone else is watching over my investments and will notify me if I need to make any changes."

"It gives me confidence when my advisor confirms that I'm still on track with my plan."

"I have peace of mind knowing that someone I trust will be there to help my wife if I'm not here."

"I could do this myself, but I just don't want to spend the time on it. And I'm sure I couldn't do it as well as a professional who spends all their time at it."

"I'd just rather be doing other things."

These are all great reasons to hire an advisor. I especially like the last one. It speaks to what retirement is all about.

Is constantly managing your W/D strategy and investment portfolio how you want to spend your retirement? Wouldn't you rather be exploring the great possibilities that life on the retirement mountain has to offer? Good. Then put this book down, hire an advisor, and go enjoy your retirement.

Citations and References

Chapter 1

1 By Mail Foreign Service
Last updated at 10:56 PM on 28th August 2009
Read more: http://www.dailymail.co.uk/news/worldnews/
article-1209638/Scientists-baffled-suicidal-cows-throw-
cliff-Switzerland.html

2 http://www.ksee24.com/news/local/53512477.html
More than 30 cows fall to their death over cliff
Updated Aug 17, 2009 at 5:25 PM PDT

3 Danger: Beware of Falling Cows
Nov 6 01:27 PM US/Eastern
MANSON, Wash. (AP)
http://www.breitbart.com/article.php?id=
d8sob4ug0&show_article=1

4 "Cattle Handling Pointers" by R. Gill, C. Pate, and R. Machen
"Cattle can see everywhere but directly behind them
or a small blind spot in front of them."
http://admin.aghost.net/images/E0110901/
CattleHandlingPointersBCSC08.pdf

5 The EBRI Retirement Readiness Rating:™ Retirement Income Preparation and Future Prospects
EBRI Issue Brief #344 (July 2010)
Paperback, 36 pp.
PDF, 1,452 kb
Employee Benefit Research Institute, 2010
http://www.ebri.org/publications/ib/index.
cfm?fa=ibDisp&content_id=4593

Chapter 2

1 EBRI, Trends in Early Retirement, July 2001
http://www.ebri.org/publications/facts/index.
cfm?fa=0701fact

2 http://www.pgcalc.com/pdf/twolife.pdf
http://www.72t.net/Calculators/LifeExpectancy

3 "Mortality". Britannica.com.
http://www.britannica.com/EBchecked/topic/393100/
mortality. Retrieved 2010-11-04.

4 A population history of North America
By Michael R. Haines, Richard Hall Steckel, Cambridge
University Press, c2000
Page 79

5 CDC/NCHS
http://www.cdc.gov/nchs/data/hus/hus2009tables/
Table024.pdf

Chapter 3

**1 http://www.foodtimeline.org/foodfaq5.
html#mcdonalds**

2 Annual Inflation
Is inflation rising or falling?
Updated 1/14/2011
Inflationdata.com
http://inflationdata.com/inflation/Inflation/
AnnualInflation.asp

Chapter 6

1 The EBRI Retirement Readiness Rating:™ Retirement Income Preparation and Future Prospects
EBRI Issue Brief #344 (July 2010)
Paperback, 36 pp.
PDF, 1,452 kb
Employee Benefit Research Institute, 2010

2 Simple Wealth, Inevitable Wealth
By Nick Murray, Fourth Edition: Thanksgiving 2010
The Nick Murray Company
www.nickmurray.com

Chapter 7

1 http://www.economist.com/node/17722567
The U-bend of life
Why, beyond middle age, people get happier
as they get older
The Economist
Dec 16th 2010 | from PRINT EDITION

2 Can Money Buy Happiness? Gallup Poll Asks, and the World Answers
ScienceDaily (July 2, 2010)
http://www.sciencedaily.com/
releases/2010/07/100701072652.htm

Chapter 8

1 Dow Jones Industrial Average℠
is published by and proprietary to Dow Jones indexes,
a licensed trademark and the marketing name of CME
Group Index Services LLC, and have been licensed for use.
"Dow Jones®", "Dow Jones Indexes", "Dow Jones Industrial
Average℠ are service marks of Dow Jones Trademark
Holdings, LLC. "CME" is a trademark of Chicago Mercantile
Exchange Inc. All content of the Dow Jones Industrial
Average℠ © CME Group Index Services LLC 2011.

Chapter 10

1 NOAA/NWS Glossary
http://www.nws.noaa.gov/glossary/index.php?letter=w

2 Based upon monte carlo analysis conducted with Quantext
Portfolio Planner V4.0 software, Quantext, Inc.. Zones based
upon joint life expectancy, with spouses of same age.

Chapter 11

1 No increase in Social Security benefits for second year
USA Today
http://www.usatoday.com/money/perfi/retirement/2010-10-
15-social-security-cola_N.htm

Chapter 13

1 Climber, 76, is oldest person ever to summit Everest after
exhaustion forces Sir Ranulph Fiennes to quit second
attempt
By Daily Mail Reporter
Last updated at 5:08 PM on 25th May 2008
http://www.dailymail.co.uk/news/article-1021657/Climber-
76-oldest-person-summit-Everest-exhaustion-forces-Sir-
Ranulph-Fiennes-quit-second-attempt.html